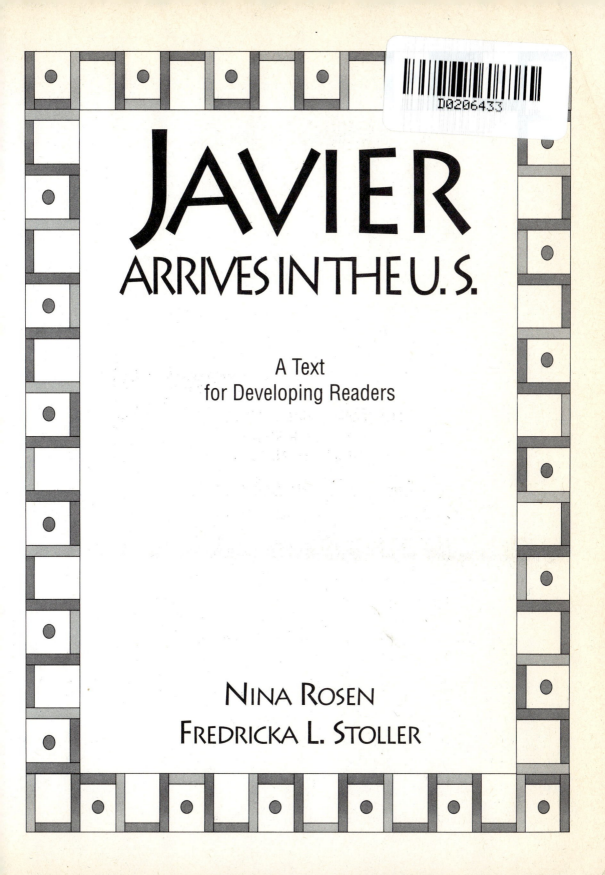

JAVIER
ARRIVES IN THE U.S.

A Text
for Developing Readers

NINA ROSEN
FREDRICKA L. STOLLER

Rosen, Nina.
    Javier arrives in the U.S. : a text for developing readers / Nina Rosen,
Fredricka L. Stoller.
        p. cm.
ISBN 0-13-512120-5
    1. Readers—United States. 2. United States—Civilization—Problems., exercises.
3. English language—Textbooks for foreign speakers. I. Stoller, Fredricka. II.
Title. III. Title: Javier arrives in the U.S. IV. Title: Javier arrives in the United
States.
PE1127.H5R67   1994   93-45483
428.6'4—dc20

Acquisitions editor: Nancy L. Leonhardt
Editorial production/design manager: Dominick Mosco
Editorial/production supervision
 and interior design: Christine McLaughlin Mann
Production Coordinator: Ray Keating

Cover Design Coordinator: Merle Krumper
Cover Design: Rosemarie Paccione
Electronic Art: Todd Ware

Interior Art: O-Lan Jones and Wanda España

© 1994 by PRENTICE HALL REGENTS
Prentice-Hall, Inc.
A Paramount Communication Company
Englewood Cliffs, New Jersey 07632

Printed on Recycled Paper

Printed in the United States of America

10 9 8 7 6 5 4 3

ISBN 0-13-512120-5

Prentice-Hall International (UK) Limited, *London*
Prentice-Hall of Australia Pty. Limited, *Sydney*
Prentice-Hall Canada Inc., *Toronto*
Prentice-Hall Hispanoamericana, S.A., *Mexico*
Prentice-Hall of India Private Limited, *New Delhi*
Prentice-Hall of Japan, Inc., *Tokyo*
Simon & Schuster Asia Pte. Ltd., *Singapore*
Editora Prentice-Hall do Brasil, Ltda., *Rio de Janeiro*

Dedicated to Our Immigrant Grandmothers,
Estelle Leedy and Bella Siegel,
Who Were Unacknowledged ESL Students

Table of Contents

Acknowledgments

We gratefully acknowledge our ESL students, the real Javier and other students like him, from a variety of school settings; they have told us their stories, discussed the challenges which slowed their progress as newcomers to the US, and described the strategies they employed to be successful in their new lives. We are honored to be able to share many of their personal trials and triumphs with other ESL readers in this textbook.

Our gratitude also goes to the ESL teachers who spent countless hours in their classrooms piloting these materials, then providing us with their feedback. A special thank you goes to Camille Stewart of Lindhurst High School, Olivehurst, CA, who piloted these materials with a number of her ESL classes. During the early stages of the book, Camille's students, who couldn't wait for the next "installment," wrote their own chapters for the book. We hope other students will be equally engaged.

We would also like to thank Jan Jones of Bethune Junior High School, Los Angeles, CA, for her excellent suggestions as well as the thoughtful advice provided by her junior high students. Susan Tarne of Glendale Community College, Adult Community Training Center, Glendale, CA, and her students provided us with valuable feedback that enabled us to strengthen the "adult perspective" in the story. In addition, we thank Courtney and Kristin Lowe for their help with various exercises.

Special thanks to Eric Bredenberg, at Prentice Hall Regents, for his continued support and faith in this project, and to Tom Dare, for his enthusiasm and encouragement. And our thanks to Nancy Leonhardt, our Acquisitions Editor, who has ushered the manuscript through all the hoops necessary for Javier to reach ESL students in their classrooms.

Finally, we would like to thank our families—Richard Rosen, Lola, Sasha, Katrina, and Bill Grabe—for being so supportive, patient, and accepting of Javier who became a member of our families.

To the Teacher

Javier Arrives in the U.S. is both an ESL reader and a reading skills development book. It combines a highly motivating fictional story with a wide array of reading exercises that provide practice in effective reading skills, critical thinking, and problem resolution. Instead of a series of unrelated vignettes, *Javier Arrives in the U.S.* is presented as a continuous story line that allows students to get involved with the text: it is about them, about their transitional experience as immigrants and the challenges they face in a new setting. Each chapter leaves students in anticipation of what will happen next in the life of Javier. The story reflects real life topics of interest to young adults new in America—romance, cars, school, friends, conflict. These topics allow students to bring an existing schema to the reading setting which, in turn, aids them in the successful development of reading skills. They have an opportunity to interact with their peers when discussing familiar topics; at the same time, they are developing valuable academic reading skills.

Javier Arrives in the U.S. is based on the lives of our own students. The familiar, yet gripping, story line and built-in contextualization make language in the story both comprehensible and engaging, while evoking the visual imagery of the immigrant transition. The universal theme can be enjoyed by mixed ethnicities at junior and senior high school levels as well as the adult level.

Javier Arrives in the U.S. is ideal material for the ESL classroom, the reading class, the pull-out situation, and the content class. Through the evocative storyline, students are drawn in and as they read, they are exposed to reading skills expected in mainstream courses, and indeed, in the real world. Skills of synthesis and analysis of information, recall of previously encountered/learned information, and evaluation are all incorporated into a wide range of exercises. Through extended involvement, students view reading as a pleasurable activity, one in which they experience success and the sense of being a reader.

After completing all the chapters and accompanying exercises, students have an opportunity to engage in an authentic pleasure reading experience by reading "The Whole Story." They read *Javier* again, only this time as a novela without exercises, simply for enjoyment.

We hope this book will reach out to those students who have been unable to enjoy reading because it has not been relevant to their lives.

If they are able to become engaged in the experience, language will expand and self-esteem will be enhanced as students learn that they are not alone in the struggle for personal success.

Using the Exercises and Activities

The exercises in this book will help your students become better readers. There are exercises that address general and academic reading skills and strategies as well as real life skills. You'll recognize familiar as well as new exercises; the variety is intended to encourage students to go beyond rote, mechanical learning and become engaged, active readers in the process.

Each chapter has **Previewing exercises** to be completed before students read the story; these exercises bring students *into* the text by helping them access background information that facilitates comprehension of the text. The **Careful reading** section takes students through the story and encourages extended reading. **Post-reading exercises** take them *beyond* the text by checking students' comprehension and requiring them to extend and apply what they know and have learned.

Students are asked to read the text silently. When doing the pre- and post-reading exercises, students work in pairs or groups in order to discuss what they are reading, thus activating and reinforcing new language and concepts.

The exercises described below are included in the majority of chapters. We offer a rationale for the exercises and some teaching suggestions to enhance the reading experience provided by the teacher.

Learn about your book: This introductory section—to be completed before students start Chapter One—serves three important functions. It is designed a) to familiarize students with the format of the book; b) to help students predict the contents of the book, building up expectations and excitement about reading the story; and c) to introduce students to a pre-reading technique employed by skilled readers whereby readers examine the organization of a book while becoming familiar with the general contents before starting to read.

Previewing exercises: A variety of previewing exercises are incorporated into the text; they can be easily used by teachers to introduce each chapter. The exercises are intended to bring students into the story by activating background knowledge and relating it to the text. When students a) examine the title and illustration of the chapter, b) skim for main ideas, c) scan for details, d) sequence events, and/or e) predict the contents of each chapter, they are preparing for successful reading.

Each chapter begins with an illustration and several short-answer questions that require students to utilize background knowledge to predict the general contents of the chapter. While sharing responses with the teacher and classmates, students learn from one another, creating a shared body of knowledge that enhances their comprehension of the text. Remember to time (or have students time) skimming and scanning exercises. Giving students a time limit (e.g., two minutes) to complete a skimming exercise will oblige students to truly skim rather than read slowly and carefully.

Because readers understand what they read by relating it to what they already know, it is well worth the time to preview each chapter. Spend enough time previewing to tap students' background knowledge while leaving sufficient time for careful reading and post-reading exercises.

Careful reading: After completing the previewing activities for each chapter, students have the chance to read the text silently and carefully. Careful reading enables students to develop habits necessary for skilled reading while simultaneously getting " hooked" on the story. Although the time required for reading may vary from student to student, it is important that a significant portion of the reading be done in class; in this way, all students have an opportunity for "time on task." Teachers can model the habits of a skilled reader by also engaging in silent reading.

Understanding the text: *What did you understand?*: These exercises, presented in different formats, check students' comprehension of the text. Remember to encourage students to be active readers. When appropriate, ask students to return to the text to identify the location of their answers. In this way, students obtain extra practice in scanning and are actively engaged in the reading process.

Pay attention to students' responses. Mistakes may serve as a guide to those sections of the text which need further clarification.

Interpreting the text: *What else did you understand?:* To help students develop critical reading skills, encourage them to read between the lines and make inferences. When reviewing students' answers, ask students "How do you know?" Let students return to the text to identify information that helped them arrive at their conclusions. Since inferencing is often difficult in a new language, allow time for discussion.

What do you think?: By encouraging students to connect their own personal experiences and opinions to the text, the storyline becomes more relevant to students' lives. Answers to the questions are not in the book; rather, they are generated by the students. Therefore, allow students to explore and discover their own ideas while completing these exercises. Because there are no right or wrong answers, students may be asked to defend their answers with examples or further explanation. Such language expansion activities provide students with an opportunity to use newly acquired vocabulary and concepts in context.

Building your vocabulary: These exercises provide students with an opportunity to review and acquire new vocabulary. Exercises focus on synonyms, antonyms, homonyms, phrasal verbs, noun phrases, and descriptive adjectives. Semantic word group exercises enable students to recognize relationships among groups of words, facilitating retention and appropriate contextual use.

Students are helped by multiple exposures to new words. Recycle important words and phrases by incorporating them into other classroom activities and homework, on your bulletin boards, and in classroom discussions.

Real life skills: These exercises connect story-related incidents and themes to the real lives of your students. While developing as readers, your students will also be preparing themselves for out-of-class realities.

Thinking about the past: Students review past events in the book and/or relate personal experiences to the text when completing these exercises. Sequencing and summarizing activities provide students with opportunities to develop higher level thinking skills which, in turn, improve their reading and writing.

Thinking about the future: *Let's predict:* Being able to make predictions is fundamental to successful reading. These exercises allow students to apply information they have derived from the text to future events.

Thinking about geography: When completing these exercises, students connect events from the text to their multi-cultural classrooms and communities. Whenever possible, use a world map so that students can connect names and places with actual locations. During the world map activity in Chapter Three, you may want to post students' names with their countries and/or cities of origin on a map. You may also want to include Javier's name and the names of other characters from the book on the map.

Word recognition exercises: There are three Word Recognition Exercises for each chapter in a separate section of the book. Unlike vocabulary expansion exercises, these exercises help students learn to react rapidly and accurately to the visual image of words that appear in each chapter. We have included these exercises because research indicates that accurate, rapid, and automatic recognition skills often distinguish skilled readers from less skilled readers. In addition, comprehension problems may be the result of poor word recognition abilities.

Use the ***Let's Practice*** exercise at the beginning of the section to introduce your students to general procedures. Have your students follow this easy seven-step process:

1. start when the teacher says to begin, ideally when the second hand of the classroom clock is at "12";
2. look at the key word in the left-hand column;
3. move eyes to the right as quickly as possible to identify the identical word;
4. cross out the identical word and then quickly go to the next line;
5. when finished, look up at the clock and record exact time (in seconds and/or minutes) at the bottom of the page;
6. correct exercise and mark down the number of correct answers at the bottom of the page;
7. record progress on the progress chart at the end of the section.

For optimal results, students should complete the three recognition exercises consecutively. Use the first exercise as a warm-up; students then strive to proceed faster and more accurately while completing the second and third exercises. These exercises can be completed in a limited amount of classroom instruction time. Have students monitor their progress on the progress chart provided at the end of the section.

Word Recognition Exercises are a lot of fun for students. Students can set goals for themselves while gaining speed and accuracy with each chapter. Help students understand that as they strive to improve accuracy and speed, their scores will likely fluctuate. That is, as students improve their speed, their accuracy may falter. Similarly, when trying to improve accuracy, the time students need to complete the exercise may increase. It is acceptable to make "mistakes" when trying to increase their speed; when students obtain a perfect score (20/20), encourage them to work faster the next round of exercises with the understanding that this may lead to "mistakes."

Basically, the goal is to improve both speed and accuracy over an extended period of time; teacher and students need to realize that scores fluctuate as students strive to meet this goal.

The Whole Story: Rarely do ESL students have the opportunity to read a book from start to finish without interruption. Research suggests that students who read the same material more than once, for a variety of purposes, benefit significantly. Give your students that opportunity by having them read "The Whole Story" after completing Chapters 1-14. We suggest that your students spend extended periods of time to read "The Whole Story." Because students are familiar with the plot and characters, they will be motivated to continue extended reading both in and out of your class.

Supplementary Activities

Read chapters aloud to your students. The benefits of listening to one's teacher reading aloud are many: a) a good story well told is likely to motivate students; the teacher can animate the story and thus build student involvement; b) the teacher can add extra information that will be of interest to the students and/or clarify parts of the text that seem to puzzle students; c) students can associate the sound of a new word with the written image of the word; and d) the teacher can show interest in the story, thus motivating the students.

Encourage students to keep a journal or engage in other writing assignments that allow them to recall, relive, and/or reflect on personal experiences that are similar to those read in the text.

Consider asking students to write chapters of their own that describe the lives of other characters from the book or have students write a description of one of the illustrations in the text. These writing assignments will facilitate the use of familiar and newly acquired vocabulary in context and allow students to practice their descriptive writing and analytical skills.

Ask students to write an alternate plot or extension of the story.

Incorporate the reading skills introduced in Javier into other components of your classroom instruction. Include previewing and post-reading activities that oblige students to infer, predict, compare, synthesize, apply, evaluate, etc. Share these ideas with other teachers; they, too, can ask students to preview textbooks and pose questions that will help students develop critical thinking skills.

To the Student

This book is for you. It is a story that was told to us by a real student named Javier. Some of the facts have been changed because Javier and his family and friends asked us to change them. Javier has told his story. He wants other students to read his story. When you read the book, you will learn that everybody faces new challenges when they arrive in a new place for the first time. What is important is how we face these challenges. One thing that was helpful to Javier was school. His friends and teachers at school helped Javier overcome many obstacles and be successful. Learning to be a good student and a good reader helped him, too.

We hope you enjoy reading about Javier and his friends. We also hope that the book will help you become a strong reader. We would like to hear from you. Please write to us and let us know your thoughts, opinions or questions about Javier. Good luck!

Nina Rosen and Fredricka L. Stoller

Learn About Your Book

1. What is the title of the book?_____

2. Who are the authors? _____

3. Find the Table of Contents and answer the questions below:

    a. How many chapters are in the book?_____

    b. On what page does Chapter Seven begin? _____

    c. Which chapter begins on page 135?

    d. What is the title of the third chapter?

    _____

    _____

    e. In what chapter will you meet Javier's girlfriend? _____

    f. What is Chapter Five about?

    _____

    _____

4. What kind of exercises are at the end of the book? _____

5. What kind of certificate is at the end of the book?_____

6. How long do you think it will take you to read this book and finish the exercises?

    _____

    _____

7. Look at the pictures below. The pictures tell something about the story of Javier. What do you think the book is about?

Javier in Jalisco

The title of this book is *Javier Arrives in the U.S.* Think about the title. Look at the picture on this page.

- ◆ **Where is young Javier?**
- ◆ **How old do you think Javier is?**
- ◆ **Who is Javier with?**

Previewing: Skimming for Main Ideas

What is Chapter One about? Before you read the chapter carefully, **skim** Chapter One to find the **main ideas**. The main idea is the **most important idea**. Each paragraph has a main idea. Match the main idea listed below with the paragraph number. When you skim, work quickly!

a. _____ Javier prepares for a trip to the U.S.A.

b. _____ Javier and his sister live with their grandmother.

c. _____ Javier's parents plan to move from Mexico to California.

d. _____ Javier waves good-bye to his parents.

e. _____ Javier and his sister have many friends.

f. _1_ This story is about Javier.

g. _____ Javier misses his parents.

h. _____ Javier's father gave him a gift.

i. _____ Javier dreams of the U.S.A.

What Do You Know About Chapter One Now?

◆ Does Javier live in Mexico or in the United States?
◆ Do his parents live in Mexico or in the United States?
◆ Does Javier live with his grandmother or with his aunt?
◆ Is Javier going to go to the United States?

Careful reading: Now read Chapter One carefully.

Javier in Jalisco

1   This is the story of Javier.[1] Javier was born in Guadalajara,[2] a city in Jalisco,[3] Mexico. Javier lived with his mother and father, his grandmother, and his younger sister, Ana. They all lived together in a small, adobe[4] house. The house was surrounded by many large, green trees. The sun filled the house with light. The wind made the house nice and cool.

2   When Javier was five years old, his mother and father moved to Los Angeles, California. They left Javier and his sister with Abuelita,[5] their grandmother. Javier's parents told him that they were going to California to find a better life for the whole family. Javier did not understand. He was too young. He was sad to say good-bye to his parents. Señor[6] Flores took Javier for a walk before he went to California. He gave him a small knife with a pearl handle.

3   "Here is a gift, son," he said. "I'll see you soon. Your mother and I will send for you as soon as we can." Señor Flores gave Javier a hug. "Everyone is depending on you and your sister. Be a good son."

4   That night, Javier and Ana waved good-bye to their mother and father. Javier's mother and father started their journey to Los Angeles.

5   In Jalisco, Javier lived a good life with his grandmother. Javier loved his abuelita. He always tried to help her in the house. Each morning he woke up

---

1 **Javier:** / ha-vee-yer /; a man's name. In English, Xavier
2 **Guadalajara:** / gwad-uh-la-ha-ra /; a city in the state of Jalisco
3 **Jalisco:** / ha-lee-sko /; a state in Mexico
4 **adobe:** / uh-do-bee /; earthen clay used for making houses and pottery
5 **abuelita:** / a-bway-lee-ta /; Spanish for grandmother
6 **señor:** / sen-yor /; Spanish for Mr. or sir

early and went outside to feed the chickens in the yard. Then he went back into the house and washed his hands and face. He ate his breakfast of bread and warm milk, said good-bye to Abuelita and walked with his sister, Ana, to school.

6   At school, Javier and Ana had many friends. They all laughed and talked together. The maestra[7] greeted them at the door. Life was happy for Javier and his sister. Javier always felt comfortable at home with his family and at school with his friends.

7   Nine years passed. Javier still missed his parents, but he was growing up. His parents visited him at Christmas time every year. He was accustomed to living with his grandmother. He often received letters from his mother and father. Sometimes his parents sent packages with clothes and toys. He was waiting to go to California to see his parents.

8   Javier dreamed about life in the United States. He wondered about the U.S.A., a foreign country, where people spoke English.

9   One sunny day, Javier returned from school. He found a letter from his father, Señor Flores. The letter said that it was time for Javier and Ana to come to Los Angeles. Javier was very happy. He began to prepare for his trip. He thought about his new life in the United States.

7 **maestra:** / ma-ace-tra /; Spanish for teacher

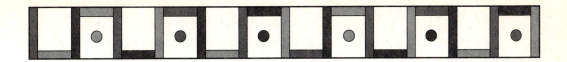

Understanding the Text

What did you understand?

Think about Chapter One. Are the following statements TRUE (T) or FALSE (F)?

a. _____ Javier was born in the U.S.

b. _____ Javier missed his parents.

c. _____ Javier lived with his grandmother and brother in Mexico.

d. _____ Javier's father and mother went to spend their money in the U.S.

e. _____ Javier's family wanted a better life.

f. _____ Javier's father wanted Javier to be a good son.

g. _____ Señor Flores gave Javier a gift before leaving.

Interpreting the Text

*What **else** did you understand?*

Are these statements TRUE (T) or FALSE (F)? How do you know?

a. _____ Javier's parents were worried about money.

b. _____ Javier was popular in school.

c. _____ Javier was twelve years old when he went to the U.S.

d. _____ Javier's parents worked in the U.S.

e. _____ Señor Flores is Javier's father.

What Do You Think?

Discuss these questions with your classmates. Use your own ideas. The answers are not in the chapter.

1. Señor Flores told Javier, "Everyone is depending on you and your sister. Be a good son." (paragraph 3)

    a. Why did Señor Flores say, "Be a good son"?

    _____

    _____

    b. How did Javier's life change after his parents left?

    _____

    _____

2. Javier's parents told him that they were going to California to find a better life for the whole family. (paragraph 2)

    a. How do you think their lives might be better in California?

    _____

    _____

    b. How do you think their lives might be more difficult in California?

    _____

    _____

3. Javier's parents worked for nine years in the U.S. before sending for Javier and Ana. (paragraph 7)

    a. Why do you think they waited so long?

    _____

    _____

b. Javier's parents left Mexico when Javier was 5 years old. Now Javier is 14 years old. In what ways will it be difficult for a 14 year-old boy to move to a new country?

_____

_____

Thinking About the Past

Write down answers to these questions. Then discuss your answers with a classmate.

1. Javier lived in Mexico before going to the United States. Where did you live before you came to the United States?

_____

_____

2. Javier lived with his grandmother and sister in Mexico. He lived with his parents and sister in the United States. Who did you live with before you came to the United States? Who do you live with now?

_____

_____

3. Javier dreamed about life in the United States. He wondered about the people who spoke English. What dreams did you have about the United States before you came?

_____

_____

4. Javier's mother and father went to the United States first. After nine years, they sent for Javier and his sister, Ana. Did anyone in your family come to the United States first? Who? Why did they come? Why did you come?

_____

_____

Thinking About the Future

Let's Predict

Javier and Ana are preparing to go to Los Angeles, California. They will join their parents. How do you think they are going to feel when they arrive in Los Angeles?

Look at the words listed below. Which words describe how Javier or Ana might feel in Los Angeles? Draw faces in the circles to describe those feelings.

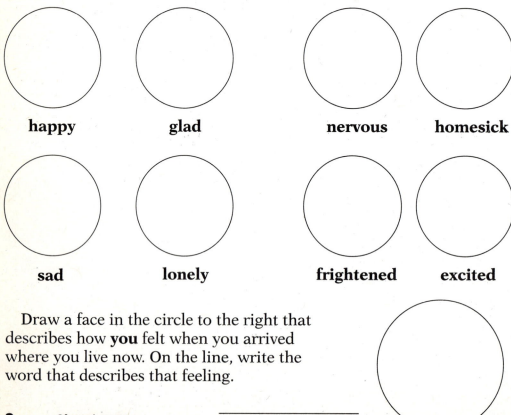

happy   **glad**   **nervous**   **homesick**

sad   **lonely**   **frightened**   **excited**

Draw a face in the circle to the right that describes how **you** felt when you arrived where you live now. On the line, write the word that describes that feeling.

_____

Building Your Vocabulary

Synonyms

Many words have *similar* (almost the same) meanings; these words are called *synonyms*. Consider some synonyms that you know and use every day:

big = large   hard = difficult

Fill in the crossword puzzle with the synonyms of the words below. You can find the synonyms in Chapter One. Read the paragraph in parenthesis to find the synonym.

Across

2 mother and father (paragraph 2)
4 trip (paragraph 4)
6 big (paragraph 1)
8 began (paragraph 4)

Down

1 everybody (paragraph 3)
3 little (paragraph 1)
5 a lot (paragraph 1)
7 present (paragraph 3)

2 Arrival

Look at the title of this chapter. Then look at the illustration.

- ◆ **Where is Javier now?**
- ◆ **How do you think Javier traveled from Jalisco to California?**
- ◆ **What does Javier see on the streets of this new city?**
- ◆ **How is Javier's new home in California different from his home in Jalisco?**
- ◆ **What do you think this chapter is going to be about?**

Previewing: Skimming for Main Ideas

What is Chapter Two about? Before reading Chapter Two, read the list of main ideas below. Each paragraph in Chapter Two has a **main idea**. Match the **main idea** listed below with the paragraph number. Work quickly!

a. _____ Javier needs to learn English.

b. _*1*_ Javier wakes up in the United States.

c. _____ Javier gets out of bed and looks outside.

d. _____ Javier feels lonely in Los Angeles.

Previewing: Scanning for Details

Look at the list of phrases below. All these phrases are in Chapter Two. Can you find the phrases in the chapter? Which paragraph are they in? **Scan** the chapter to find the answers. When you find the phrases in the story, write the paragraph number on the line. Work quickly!

a. _*3*_ learn English

b. _____ strange feeling

c. _____ noisy cars

d. _____ early morning sun

e. _____ old house in Mexico

f. _____ big, shady trees

g. _____ full of freeways

h. _____ a big hurry

i. _____ feel lonely

Careful reading: Now read Chapter Two carefully.

Arrival

1   Javier woke up. He did not remember where he was. Everything around him was strange. He lay in bed with a sleepy feeling. Slowly he remembered that he was in the United States. He had dreamed about the United States for a long time. He was really here. He took a deep breath and the smell made him certain; it smelled so different from the old house in Mexico. A small window let in the early morning sun.

2   Javier got out of bed quietly and went outside. Everything looked different, so different. At home there were big, shady trees, and fruit trees and places where he was able to see for miles and miles. Here, the houses were crowded close together, the streets were busy with noisy cars moving very quickly. Everyone was in a big hurry.

3   "So this is Los Angeles," Javier thought. "It is a place full of freeways, cars, and people. And I'll bet that everyone speaks English." Javier had a strange feeling in his stomach. He knew that he wanted to learn English. He knew that English could help him be successful in the U.S.A.

4   Javier went back inside the house. He sat down on the sofa. He was thinking. "I have just arrived. I feel lonely. I must wait and see what happens. Maybe I'll like it here but maybe I won't."

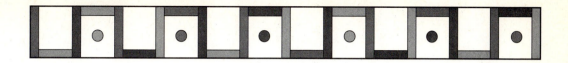

Understanding the Text

What did you understand?

Think about Chapter Two. Are the following statements TRUE (T) or FALSE (F)?

a. _____ Javier is in the United States with his two brothers.

b. _____ Javier feels lonely in Los Angeles.

c. _____ Javier is sure he will like his new life.

d. _____ Javier lives in a crowded neighborhood now.

e. _____ Javier's home in Los Angeles is the same as his home in Jalisco.

Interpreting the Text

*What **else** did you understand?*

Are these statements TRUE (T) or FALSE (F)? How do you know? If you are not sure, write MAYBE (M).

a. _____ There wasn't much traffic in Jalisco, Mexico.

b. _____ There are many fruit trees growing outside Javier's home in Los Angeles.

c. _____ Javier is worried about learning English.

d. _____ Javier brought his pocketknife with him.

e. _____ Javier misses his friends in Jalisco.

What Do You Think?

Discuss these questions with your classmates. Use your own ideas. The answers are not in the chapter.

1. When Javier looked around, he noticed that everyone was in a big hurry in Los Angeles.   (paragraph 2)

   a. Why is everybody in such a hurry?

   _____

   _____

   b. Where do you think everyone is going?

   _____

   _____

   c. Were people in a hurry in your native country? native city? Explain.

   _____

   _____

2. Javier said he had a strange feeling in his stomach.   (paragraph 3)

   a. Why did he have a strange feeling in his stomach?

   _____

   _____

   b. Have you ever had a strange feeling in your stomach? When? Why?

   _____

   _____

3. Javier said that English could help him be successful in the U.S.A. (paragraph 3)

   a. What opportunities will Javier have when he learns English?

   _____

   _____

   b. Do you think it will be difficult for Javier to learn English? Why? Why not?

   _____

   _____

Let's Compare

Javier noticed that everything looked different when he arrived in Los Angeles (paragraph 2). What did he see in Los Angeles that was new?

Fill in the boxes below. Which words best describe Guadalajara? Which words best describe Los Angeles?

fruit trees   rushed people   open markets
crowded houses   good views   big supermarkets
big, shady trees   heavy traffic   video stores
noisy cars   modern skyscrapers   adobe homes

Guadalajara	Los Angeles
	big supermarkets

Think about the places where you have lived. Are they different? Fill in these boxes with images you have of each place.

I lived in _____	I now live in _____

Thinking About the Future

Let's Predict

1. Javier said, "Maybe I'll like it here but maybe I won't."
   (paragraph 4)

   What do you think Javier will like? What do you think he'll dislike?
   Make a list below.

Javier will like . . .	Javier will dislike . . .
donuts *nintendo*	*smog*

2. What do you like in *your* new city? What do you dislike?

I like . . .	I dislike . . .

Thinking About Geography

	City	State	Country
◆ Where was Javier when he was a little boy?			
◆ Where is Javier now?			
◆ Where do *you* live now?			
◆ Where did *you* live before?			
◆ Where is your school?			

Where do your classmates come from? Ask eight classmates and fill in the chart.

Classmates' names	City	State	Country
1.			
2.			
3.			
4.			
5.			
6.			
7.			
8.			

Building Your Vocabulary

Antonyms

Many words have *opposite* meanings; these words are called *antonyms*. Consider some antonyms that you know and use every day:

old/new   young/old   tall/short   thin/fat   like/dislike

Fill in the crossword puzzle with the **antonyms** of the words below. You can find the antonyms in Chapter Two. Read the paragraph in parentheses to find the antonym.

Across

3 outside (paragraph 4)
8 forget (paragraph 1)
9 uncertain (paragraph 1)
10 big (paragraph 1)

Down

1 quiet (paragraph 2)
2 new (paragraph 1)
4 familiar (paragraph 1)
5 late (paragraph 1)
6 slowly (paragraph 2)
7 unable (paragraph 2)

A Reunion with Papa 3

Read the title of this chapter and look at the illustration.
- ◆ **Where is Javier?**
- ◆ **Who is Javier talking to?**
- ◆ **Does Javier look sad? happy? confused? worried?**
- ◆ **What do you think they are talking about?**

Thinking About the Past

Sequencing Events

Think about Chapters One and Two. What happened first (1st)? What happened second (2nd); third (3rd); fourth (4th); fifth (5th); sixth (6th); seventh (7th); and eighth (8th)? When you answer, use the correct word.

_____ Javier says good-bye to his grandmother.

_____ Javier notices how different California life is.

_____ Javier gets a letter from his parents.

____*first*___ Javier's family lives together in Mexico.

_____ Javier decides he needs to learn English.

_____ Javier prepares for a trip to the U.S.

_____ Javier waves good-bye to his parents.

Thinking About the Future

Let's Predict

The list below describes events that will happen in Chapter Three. What do you think will happen first (1st); second (2nd); third (3rd); fourth (4th)? When you answer, write in the numbers.

____*1st*___ Javier is worried about going to school in the U.S.

_____ Javier talks to his father about his worries.

_____ Señor Flores gives Javier good advice.

_____ Señor Flores listens to Javier carefully.

Careful reading: Read Chapter Three carefully. Think about the advice that Señor Flores gives to Javier.

A Reunion with Papa

1   In the house, Javier passed the room where his mother and father were sleeping. He walked quietly because he didn't want to awaken his parents, but Señor Flores heard Javier's footsteps and softly called to Javier.

2   "Son, what is troubling you?" asked Javier's father.

"May I come in, father? I can't sleep," Javier answered.

"Tell me what is troubling you, son," said Señor Flores. Javier walked into the bedroom where his mother and father slept. He spoke softly because his mother was sleeping.

"Father, how can I go to school in this new place? I can't speak the language and I won't understand what people are saying to me."

3   "Javier," said his father kindly, "come and sit down here." Javier obeyed his father. He sat down on a chair near Señor Flores.

"Are you happy that we are all together again? Are you happy that you are in a new place?"

4   "I don't know yet, father," answered Javier honestly. "Everything is different from Jalisco. I have been thinking about the students at my new school. Do you think they'll laugh at me?"

5   "Maybe. Maybe some people will laugh at you. Your language is different, so some people might think you are different. You *sound* different. Maybe some people will laugh because they don't know what else to do. But you are not different; you simply speak a different language. You are the same person you were in Jalisco. Maybe we look a little different. We come from another place. People of all cultures move their hands in

different ways or walk in different ways. Each culture has different customs. So in some ways, in our culture, we behave differently."

6   "You will see in school," continued Señor Flores. "The people in your classes will be from other countries. They will also feel strange. Perhaps you will meet other young people from Mexico, from El Salvador, or maybe from Southeast Asia, Russia, or Poland. I know it's difficult for you to understand, but believe your Papa; all people are the same under the skin. They are here from many countries trying to learn a new language and a new culture in a new place. That's a big job."

7   Javier nodded his head and smiled. The ideas his father spoke of were new ideas. Señor Flores had many things to teach his son. Javier began to feel happy thinking about his new life. He wanted to meet the new people at school from many different countries and cultures.

8   "But remember," Señor Flores continued, "all people are the same in one way. They want to love and they want other people to love them. They hope to grow to be good. They have to work hard to be good. There are many difficulties. We fall down but we get up again. Always try to work hard, to be good and to love others. Don't forget this and then you'll understand that people who look at you strangely are not so strange."

9   "Now, show me your pocket knife," said Señor Flores. Javier took the knife out of his pocket. He always carried the knife his father had given him long ago.

"Soon I will begin to teach you how to carve wooden boxes. You are old enough now that you won't cut your fingers off!" Señor Flores laughed. Javier laughed too.

"I won't cut myself, Papa. I know how to use the knife."

"Good! Then maybe we can make boxes out of wood. But now, get ready for school. Today is your first day. Don't be late!"

10   Javier felt better. To see his father again, to hear him talk and to know that they were going to carve made Javier happy to be in the United States.

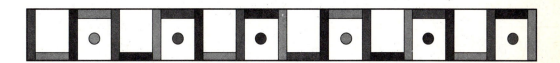

Understanding the Text

What did you understand?

Think about Chapter Three. Are the following statements TRUE (T) or FALSE (F)?

a. _____ Javier had trouble sleeping.

b. _____ Javier listened to his father carefully in the kitchen.

c. _____ Javier's new school will have students from many countries.

d. _____ Javier knows how to carve boxes.

e. _____ Javier felt better after talking to his father.

f. _____ Javier was worried before he spoke with his father.

g. _____ Javier's father did not listen to his son.

h. _____ Javier's mother gave good advice that morning.

i. _____ Javier always carries the knife his father gave him.

Interpreting the Text

*What **else** did you understand?*

Are these statments TRUE (T) or FALSE (F)? How do you know? If you are not sure, write MAYBE (M).

a. _____ Javier will look strange to his classmates.

b. _____ Javier's father can carve wood.

c. _____ Javier's father speaks English because he has been in the U.S. for nine years.

d. _____ People will laugh at Javier.

e. _____ Señor Flores is a wise man.

f. _____ Javier speaks Spanish with his parents.

What Do You Think?

Discuss these questions with your classmates. Use your own ideas. The answers are not in the chapter.

1. Señor Flores told Javier, "All people are the same under the skin."

   a. In what ways are all people the same?

   _____

   _____

   b. In what ways are people a little different?

   _____

   _____

2. Javier asked his father, "Do you think the kids in school will laugh at me?"

    a. Do you think students from other countries will laugh at Javier? Why? Why not?

    _____

    _____

    b. Why do some kids laugh at new students at school?

    _____

    _____

Thinking About Geography

Señor Flores told Javier, "Perhaps you will meet other young people from Mexico, from El Salvador, or maybe from Southeast Asia, Russia, or Poland" (paragraph 6). Where are these countries? Look at a world map.

    a. Find Mexico, El Salvador, Vietnam, Russia, and Poland.

    b. Find your native country. What other countries are nearby?

    c. Where are you now? Find that place on the map.

    d. How did you get from your native country to where you are now?

    e. Ask your teacher to show you where he/she was born.

    f. Ask your classmates where they are from. Find their countries on the map. Are their native countries **close to** or **far from** your native country?

Classmates' names	Native country	Close to or far from your native country

Thinking About the Future

Let's Predict

Today is Javier's first day in school. Answer the following questions with Yes, No, or Maybe. Put a check (✓) in the appropriate box.

	Yes	No	Maybe
◆ Is Javier worried about his first day at school?			
◆ Do you think Javier will make friends easily?			
◆ Will he like his teacher?			
◆ Will the school day be strange for him?			
◆ Will Javier feel happy at the end of the first day?			
◆ Will he understand the teacher?			

Think about *your* first day at school in the United States.

	Yes	No	Maybe
◆ Did you make a friend?			
◆ Did you like your teacher?			
◆ Were you happy at the end of the first day?			
◆ Did you understand when the teacher spoke?			

What do you remember most about your first day at school in the U.S.?

I remember _____

_____

_____

Building Your Vocabulary

Word Groups

Sometimes it is easier to learn words in groups. Look at this group of words. What do they have in common? Add other "family" words to this list.

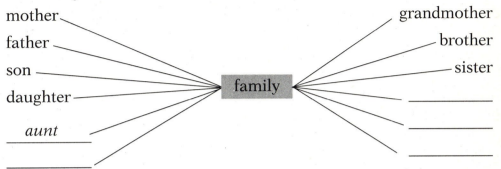

mother

father

son

daughter

aunt

_____

family

grandmother

brother

sister

_____

_____

_____

Draw Javier's family tree. Include the following names in the correct places: Señor Flores, Mrs. Flores, Javier, Ana.

Now draw your own family tree. Start with your parents' or grandparents' names at the top.

Real Life Skills

Learning from Others

A. Señor Flores gave his son **advice** before the first day of school. Señor Flores wanted to help his son. Do you understand what *advice* is?

What advice did Señor Flores give to Javier? Find at least two examples in the chapter.

Example: *Señor Flores told Javier, "Learning a new language and a new culture is a big job."*

1. _____

2. _____

3. _____

B. Did anyone give you advice before you started school?

Person	Yes	No	Person	Yes	No
a teacher	____	____	your grandparents	____	____
an older brother	____	____	a friend	____	____
an older sister	____	____	a neighbor	____	____
your parents	____	____	a cousin	____	____

1. What advice did they give you?

_____

_____

2. Did their advice help you? How?

_____

_____

C. Form a group with your classmates.

What is the best advice you can give to new students in your school? Remember: Your advice will help them be successful at school.

1. _____

_____

2. _____

_____

3. _____

_____

What is the best advice you can give to new people in your neighborhood? Remember: Your advice will help them live in your neighborhood.

1. _____

_____

2. _____

_____

3. _____

_____

School Days

Look at the chapter title and the illustration.

◆ **Where is Javier now?**

◆ **What's happening?**

◆ **What do you see in the office?**

◆ **Look at the student on the right. What does he have on his arm?**

Previewing: Scanning for Details

Before reading Chapter Four, read the questions below. **Scan** the Chapter paragraphs (in parentheses) to find the correct answers. Work quickly!

1. What did Javier have for breakfast on his first day of school?   **(1)**
   a. bread and coffee   **b.** cereal and milk   **c.** bread and milk

2. What kind of school are Javier and Ana attending?   **(2)**
   a. a public school   **b.** a private school   **c.** a religious school

3. How many students from Mexico are at Javier's school?   **(4)**
   a. a lot   **b.** a few   **c.** five

4. Who is Spider going to introduce Javier to?   **(5)**
   a. some guys   **b.** some girls   **c.** some teachers

5. What do Javier and Ana need to bring when they register for school?   **(6)**
   a. a passport   **b.** proof of vaccinations   **c.** a list of clinics

6. After leaving school, what was the Flores family waiting for? (8)
   a. a taxi   **b.** a bus   **c.** a doctor

What do you think this chapter is about?

_____

_____

Careful reading: Read Chapter Four carefully.

School Days

1   Javier got dressed and ready for school. He went into the kitchen and ate some bread and drank some milk. It was his first day of school. Javier's family went with him to school. Mr. and Mrs. Flores were taking their children to the office to register. The clerk in the office didn't speak Spanish, but she asked a student worker in the office to translate for the Flores family. The clerk gave them a lot of forms to fill out so that Javier and his sister, Ana, could attend school. The forms were in Spanish and English so Javier and Ana could read the forms and fill them out. They tried their best to finish everything. The student assistant smiled and said, "My name is Luz[8] and I'll try to help you if I can." Javier and Ana were glad the student assistant was there.

"Have you had your immunizations?" asked Luz.

2   "Our what?" asked Ana.

"Your immunizations, you know, vaccinations. You have to be immunized to attend public school here," answered Luz.

3   "You have to get your shots!" said a voice. They all looked around to see a young man about Javier's age. He was dressed in black baggy pants and a white T-shirt. He wore a bandana around his head and on his left arm there was a colorful tattoo of a spider.

"Hey, I'm Spider. They call me Spider . . . just tryin' to help."

8 **Luz:** / looz /; a woman's name; Spanish for light

"Thanks," said Javier with a grin.

Spider reached out to shake hands with Javier. He said, "I know the ropes. I've been through this stuff. Maybe I can help you out. Where're you from?"

4   "Jalisco," said Javier. "Guadalajara."

"Oh yeah? I'm from San Salvador in El Salvador. The little country with a big heart," he grinned. "So you're from Mexico. There're a lot of guys at this school from Mexico. A lot from Salvador, too. I guess we've got a whole lot of people from all over."

5   Now it was Javier's turn to say, "Oh, yeah?"

"Well, see you around. Come on down to the yard and see me. I've got a bench down there. I can introduce you to some of the guys."

"A bench?" asked Javier.

"Yeah. I'm always standing at the same bench, so now I guess it's almost mine. Everybody calls it Spider's Bench."

"Well, thanks a lot, Spider. See you."

"Yeah, thanks, Spider," added Ana.

6   "Bring in proof of your vaccinations. You need a shot for mumps, measles and rubella," Luz explained. They turned back to listen to what Luz was saying. "And you also need a TB test and a DPT shot."

"Oh, I don't know if they've had all of those," said Mrs. Flores.

"If you're missing a vaccination, here's a list of clinics you can visit for your shots. Most of the clinics are free, but some charge a fee. You can call them before you visit."

7   Luz gave Mrs. Flores the list of clinics. Mrs. Flores put it in her purse and waited as Mr. Flores stood up to leave.

"Thank you, Luz. Thank you so much," the whole family said together.

"No problem," said Luz with a smile. "Come back as soon as you've had your shots and we'll finish your registration and give you class schedules," she said, looking at Javier and Ana.

8   The Flores family said good-bye. They walked to the bus stop and waited for the bus. On the bus ride home, Mrs. Flores took out the list Luz had given her. They all studied the list, looking for a clinic that was close to their home and free of charge.

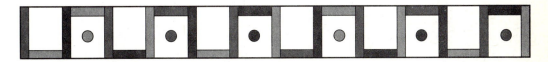

Understanding the Text

What did you understand?

Circle the correct answer to complete the sentence.

1. When Javier and his family first arrived at his new school,

    a. they went to meet Javier's teacher.

    b. they went to meet. Ana's teacher.

    c. they met Spider.

    d. they went to the office.

2. Before registering for class,

    a. Javier and Ana spoke to the principal.

    b. Javier and Ana spoke to their teachers.

    c. Javier and Ana spoke to an office clerk.

    d. Javier and Ana spoke to the school nurse.

3. **Before going to class,**
    a. Javier and Ana needed vaccinations.
    b. Javier and Ana had to buy their books.
    c. Javier and Ana needed to meet the principal.
    d. Javier and Ana met Spider in the yard.

4. **The office clerk gave Javier and Ana many forms to fill out. The forms were**
    a. in Spanish only.
    b. in English only.
    c. in Spanish and English.

5. **Luz is a (n)**
    a. office clerk.
    b. student assistant.
    c. teacher.
    d. nurse.

6. **Luz spoke**
    a. Spanish only.
    b. English only.
    c. Spanish and English.

7. **The office clerk spoke**
    a. Spanish only.
    b. English only.
    c. Spanish and English.

8. **Spider is a (n)**
    a. student worker.
    b. student.
    c. office clerk.
    d. teacher.

9. **Spider is from**
    a. El Salvador.
    b. Poland.
    c. the United States.
    d. Mexico.

10. **Spider had many friends who**
    a. were from El Salvador.
    b. met him in the yard at "his bench."
    c. had tattoos on their arms.

11. The Flores family looked at the list of clinics. They wanted to find a clinic that was

    a. close to their home.   **c.** close to the hospital.

    b. close to school.

12. The Flores family wanted to find a clinic that

    a. gave free immunizations.   **c.** only gave rubella shots.

    b. charged money for vaccinations.

    Look back at your answers. Write complete answers in the following order: Answers 1, 2, 7, 4, 3, 12. When you finish, you will have a complete paragraph. Start with the answer to 1.

When Javier and his family first arrived at his new school, _____

_____

_____

_____

_____

_____

_____

_____

_____

Interpreting the Text

*What **else** did you understand?*

l. Spider said, *"I know the ropes."* What did he mean?

    a. He knew the rules of the school.

    b. He used rope to carry his books to school.

    c. He knows how to make rope.

Do you *know the ropes* at your school?

_____

_____

2. Spider said, *"I've been through this stuff."* What did he mean?

    a. He ate too much for lunch.
    b. He liked to look at books in the library.
    c. He had to do the same things as Javier and Ana.

What stuff have you *been through* since you arrived at school?

_____

_____

3. The clerk asked Javier and Ana to *fill out* many forms. What did they have to do?

    a. carry the forms home
    b. complete the forms
    c. give the forms to Luz

What forms did you have to *fill out* when you arrived at your school?

_____

_____

4. Luz said that some clinics *charge a fee*. What did she mean?

    a. People have to pay money for shots.
    b. People get shots for free, without paying.
    c. People can get a yellow card there.

Does your clinic *charge a fee* for services?

_____

_____

What Do You Think?

Answer these questions. Use your own ideas. The answers are not in the chapter.

1. What kind of person is Spider?

_____

_____

2. What does Spiders' style of clothing tell you about him?

_____

_____

3. Spider "has a bench." What does this tell you about him?

_____

_____

4. Where do you "hang out" at your school?

_____

_____

Real Life Skills

School Checklist

What do you need to register at your school?

	Yes	No	I don't remember
Vaccinations			
DPT (Diphtheria, Pertussis, and Tetanus)			
MMR (Measles, Mumps, and Rubella)			
TB (Tuberculosis)			
Polio (Poliomyelitis)			
Proof of residence			
Parent or guardian's signature			
Other _____			

Interview a classmate. Ask the following questions. Use your classmate's name in your answer.

Example: When did you register at school?

Martin registered for school in early September last year.

1. What did you need to register at school?

_____

_____

2. How many vaccinations did you get before starting school?

_____

_____

3. Where did you get your vaccinations?

_____

_____

4. Were you charged a fee for the vaccinations?

_____

_____

5. How long did it take you to "know the ropes" at school?

_____

_____

Building Your Vocabulary

Homonyms

Many words sound the same but they are spelled differently and have different meanings; these words are called *homonyms*. Consider some homonyms that you know and use every day:

two	to	too
so	sew	

Chapter Four has homonyms for many words. Look at this example.

eight ___*ate*___ (paragraph __*1*__)

Look in Chapter Four for homonyms for these words. Where did you find the homonyms? Write down the paragraph number.

there _____ (_____)   **red** _____ (_____)

no _____ (_____)   **hear** _____ (_____)

war _____ (_____)   **sea** _____ (_____)

hole _____ (_____)   **four** _____ (_____)

Building Your Vocabulary

Synonyms

Chapter Four has many synonyms, words that are *similar* in meanings. Look at these synonyms from the chapter:

> student worker = student assistant
> grin = smile
> immunization = vaccination = shot

Read the pairs of words below. Are the words synonyms (S) or are they antonyms (A), words that are *opposite* in meaning?

__S__	finish	complete
_____	first	last
_____	glad	happy
_____	left	right
_____	clinics	medical offices
_____	home	house
_____	grin	cry
_____	stand up	sit down
_____	close	far
_____	start	begin
_____	fill out	complete
_____	best	worst
_____	shots	immunizations
_____	public	private
_____	help	assist

A Visit to the Doctor 5

Look at the chapter title and the illustration.
- ◆ **What do you think this Chapter is about?**
- ◆ **Where are Javier, his sister, and mother now?**
- ◆ **Why are they there?**
- ◆ **How long will they have to wait to see a nurse or doctor?**

Previewing: Scanning for Details

Before reading Chapter Five, complete the statements below. **Scan** the chapter paragraphs (in parentheses) to find the correct answers. Work quickly!

1. The Glenwood Clinic is (1)
   a. 3 blocks from the   **c.** 5 blocks from the Flores' home.
      Flores' home.
   b. 4 blocks from the Flores' home.

2. The Waiting Room at the Glenwood Clinic was (1)
   a. crowded.   **c.** quiet.
   b. empty.

3. Javier and Ana waited in the Waiting Room for (2)
   a. less than one hour.   **c.** 30 minutes.
   b. more than one hour.

4. The nurse was from (3)
   a. Los Angeles, California,   **c.** Guadalajara, Jalisco, Mexico.
      U.S.A.
   b. Toronto, Ontario, Canada.

5. The nurse asked Javier to (4)
   a. open his mouth.   **c.** open his eyes.
   b. put out his arm.

6. Javier weighed   (5)

    a. 123 pounds.   **c.** 130 pounds.

    b. 113 pounds.

7. The yellow cards were   (8)

    a. work permits.   **c.** school identification cards.

    b. proof of vaccinations.

8. The nurse wanted to tell Javier and Ana about Toronto   (9)

    a. when they returned   **c.** after they had their shots.
       to the clinic.

    b. after they learned more
       English.

What do you think this chapter is about? Why?

_____

_____

_____

_____

_____

Careful reading: Read Chapter Five carefully.

A Visit to the Doctor

1   The Glenwood Clinic was only five blocks from Javier's house. Javier walked there with his mother and sister. It was a small, one-story building on a quiet, residential street.

As they entered the building, Javier looked around. There were many people sitting in the Waiting Room. There were a few old people. There were also young children and babies. The Glenwood Clinic was crowded and noisy.

2   Javier gave the receptionist his and Ana's name. Then he sat down to wait with the other people. They waited for more than an hour. Finally, Javier heard the receptionist call his name.

"Javier Flores." Javier got up and went to the receptionist's window.

"Are you Javier Flores?" asked the receptionist in Spanish.

"Yes, I am," Javier replied. Javier was glad the receptionist spoke Spanish, but he wondered how he was going to learn English.

3   "Go through the door and you'll see the nurse's station on the left there," continued the receptionist.

Javier went through the door. He saw the nurse standing by a scale. The nurse put him on the scale to weigh him. And then, in English, she told him to open his mouth.

"You speak English. Are you from Los Angeles?" asked Javier trying out his English.

"No, I'm not. Actually I was born in Toronto. That's a city in Ontario, Canada."

4   Javier did not understand. He looked at her, puzzled. Then the nurse told him to open his mouth. Javier still did not understand. So the nurse pointed to her mouth and opened it.

"Aha," thought Javier. She wants me to open my mouth. At least I understand sign language. As soon as Javier opened his mouth, the nurse put a thermometer in it. He sat down. She took the thermometer out of his mouth and read it.

5   "You weigh 123 pounds and your temperature is normal. Very good," the nurse said with a smile. "Now, let's give you your shots. Roll up your sleeve."

6   Once again, Javier did not understand. Once again, the nurse showed him what to do. Javier rolled up his sleeve. Then he looked at the tray with three needles on it.

"You'll be getting three shots," the nurse explained. "Your DPT, MMR, and a TB test."

7   Javier didn't say anything. The nurse took a big needle and gave Javier a shot. It hurt! It hurt a lot! But Javier didn't make a sound. "It will be over soon," he thought.

8   Ana was weighed, had her temperature taken, and was given her shots, too. Now, they were both finished. The nurse stamped a yellow card for each of them. The yellow cards were proof of their vaccinations.

9   "Okay," said the nurse, "you're finished. Come back when you've learned more English and I'll tell you about Toronto." Javier did not move. Ana did not move, either.

10   "Oh dear. You didn't understand me, did you?" she said opening the door and motioning for them to leave.

11   Javier and Ana were surprised. They had waited for more than an hour and their shots had taken only five minutes. And they had never seen the doctor! They returned to the Waiting Room where Mrs. Flores was sitting patiently. They all left the Glenwood Clinic. Javier and Ana were glad their vaccinations were over. They walked home quietly because they each had an ache in their right arm.

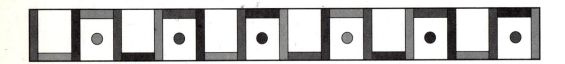

Understanding the Text

What did you understand?

Think about Chapter Five. What happened? What was the first (1st) event? the second (2nd)? the third (3rd)? the fourth (4th)? the fifth (5th)? the sixth (6th)? Use numbers in your answers.

_____   Javier and Ana waited for more than one hour. Finally the receptionist called their names.

_____   They left with their mother and walked home.

_____   After the nurse gave Javier his shots, Ana was weighed. Then she had her temperature taken, and was given her shots.

_1st_   Javier and Ana walked with their mother to the clinic. When they arrived, Javier gave the receptionist his and Ana's name.

_____   The receptionist directed Javier to the nurse's station. Then, the nurse weighed Javier and took his temperature.

_____   The nurse gave Javier and Ana their yellow cards. Then Javier and Ana went back into the Waiting Room.

Interpreting the Text

What **else** did you understand?

Read these sentences. Are they TRUE (T) or FALSE (F)? How do you know? If you are unsure, write MAYBE (M).

a. _____ The Glenwood Clinic was busy.

b. _____ The nurse had other patients who did not speak English.

c. _____ The nurse liked Javier and Ana.

d. _____ Javier and Ana had to pay for their shots.

e. _____ Javier and Ana expected to see the doctor.

f. _____ The doctor only sees sick patients.

g. _____ Javier and Ana got shots in their left arms.

h. _____ Mrs. Flores waited for Javier and Ana in the Waiting Room.

Real Life Skills

Communicating with Body Language

When Javier and Ana did not understand the nurse's words, the nurse communicated with **gestures**, that is, with body language. She did not use words. What is a gesture? What parts of your body can you use to communicate without words?

What gesture do you use to ask someone to:

stand up?	sit down?
come in?	leave?
speak louder?	be quiet?
slow down?	say hello?
say goodbye?	say okay?

Ask a classmate the following questions. Let your classmate use gestures, not words, to answer your questions.

1. How tall is your mother?
2. How big is your pet cat, your pet dog?
3. How many brothers and sisters do you have?
4. Can you count to five?
5. Can you count to ten?

Building Your Vocabulary

Word Groups

1. The Glenwood Clinic was on a *residential* street. What kinds of buildings are usually on a residential street?

   a. houses, apartment buildings, and small businesses

   b. department stores and banks

   c. supermarkets and a mall

2. Do you live in a *residential* area? Or do you live in a *commercial* area? What kinds of buildings are in your neighborhood? Circle all the buildings that are near your home.

houses	skyscrapers	a supermarket
apartment buildings	a hardware store	coffee shops
small stores	fast food restaurants	furniture stores
a department store	gas stations	a public library
a mall	the Court House	barber shops
condominiums	a bookstore	car dealers
a pet shop	laundromats	a bank
restaurants	a bakery	a video store
a health food store	liquor stores	City Hall
an art supply store	shoe stores	movie theaters
a real estate office	a newsstand	a post office
an antique store	a shoe repair shop	a bus station

3. The Glenwood Clinic is a small *one-story* building. How many floors does it have?

   a. one floor

   b. two floors

   c. three floors

4. How many *stories* does your house or apartment building have?

   a. It's one-story.

   b. It's two-stories.

   c. It's _____ stories.

5. How many *stories* does your school building have? _____

6. Look at the map of Javier's neighborhood on page 52. Javier is at home. How many blocks does he have to walk to get to

   a. school? _____   **d.** the supermarket? _____

   b. the library? _____   **e.** the newsstand? _____

   c. the post office? _____   **f.** the park? _____

7. The Glenwood Clinic is five *blocks* from Javier's house.

   a. How many blocks (or miles) is your school from your house? _____

   b. How many blocks (or miles) is the closest market from your house? _____

   c. How many blocks (or miles) is the public library from your house? _____

   d. How many blocks (or miles) is your doctor from your house? _____

8. Look at the map of Javier's neighborhood and follow these instructions:

   Javier leaves his home and turns right, going north. He walks two blocks. Then he makes a left and goes west. He walks straight ahead for two blocks. Where is he? _____

   Javier leaves his home and turns left, going south. He walks three blocks. He turns right, going west. He goes straight ahead for one block. He turns right. Where is he? _____

Real Life Skills

Giving Directions

Sit facing a classmate. Give your classmate directions to an exact location on the map of Javier's neighborhood. Start at Javier's house. (You can use a map of your own community, if you have one.) How good are your directions? Could your classmate follow your directions?

Javier's Neighborhood

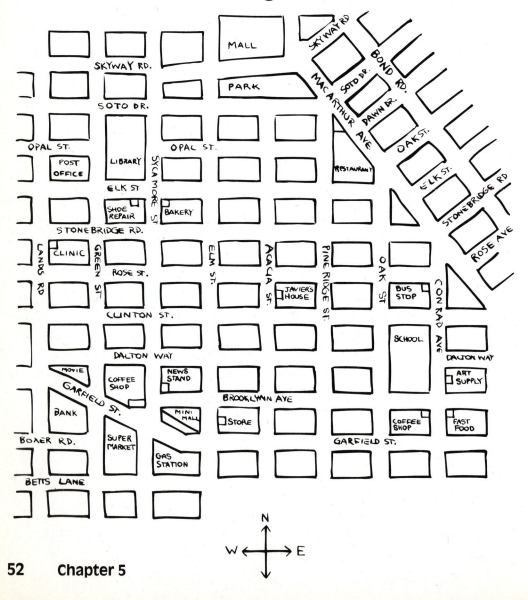

A New Romance: Guadalupe

Look at the title and illustration of this chapter. Discuss these questions with your classmates.

- ◆ **Where is Javier now?**
- ◆ **What does *romance* mean?**
- ◆ **Who do you think Javier will meet?**
- ◆ **Who is Guadalupe?**
- ◆ **What do you think this chapter will be about?**

Previewing: Skimming for Main Ideas

What is Chapter Six about? Before reading Chapter Six, read the list of main ideas below. **Skim** the chapter and match the **main idea** listed below with the correct paragraph number. Work quickly!

a. _____ Javier daydreams about Mexico.

b. _____ Javier is placed in the eleventh grade.

c. _____ Javier sees a beautiful girl in class.

d. _____ The girl's name is Guadalupe.

e. _____ Javier sees students from many countries in his class.

f. _____ Javier and the girl look at each other.

Careful reading: Read Chapter Six carefully.

A New Romance: Guadalupe

1   They placed Javier in the eleventh grade after registration. They placed Ana in the ninth grade. Javier took his class schedule and reported to his classes. As he sat in his Social Studies class, his teacher spoke English. English sounded very strange and he thought the teacher spoke very fast. He didn't understand one word.

2   In the next class, the teacher also spoke English. He thought she spoke fast, too. Javier could not pay attention. His thoughts were leading him into daydreams. He was thinking of a sunny morning in Mexico, a morning when the chickens were fighting in the yard and making a lot of loud noise.

3   As Javier daydreamed, his eyes wandered around the class. He saw the colorful posters from many countries on the wall. There were posters from all over Mexico and Central America. There were posters from Southeast Asia, Africa, Russia, and many other places he had never seen or even dreamed about. He looked at all the different students. "Where do they all come from?" he wondered. Some were from Asia. Maybe they were Korean or Japanese or Chinese. He didn't know. Other students were from different places and spoke different languages. He was looking at each face when suddenly, he stopped. He thought he was having a vision. No, it was real.

4   In the classroom sat the most beautiful angel he had ever seen. He wasn't daydreaming now. He was back in the classroom. He stared at the girl. She was sitting at a desk with a pencil in her right hand. She was writing. He could see her eyes as she looked up at the blackboard

to read the questions. Her eyes were dark and oval. She had long, thick brown hair. She didn't wear any lipstick. In fact, she wore no make-up at all. Javier could not stop staring at her.

5   The girl seemed to feel his eyes on her. She turned her head slightly. He was embarrassed because she knew he was looking at her. They both looked down. But in a moment, they both looked up again. Their eyes met. The girl turned away. Javier looked down. He tried not to look at her again. She was so beautiful. He wanted to meet her. He knew she was special.

6   The bell rang and class was over. But a new romance had begun. Javier watched the beautiful girl pick up her books. She got up and walked out of the classroom with another girl. Javier tried to stay close behind them. He wanted to hear her voice. Javier followed them as they walked out of the classroom and down the hall. The two friends were talking. Javier could not hear what they were saying, but he heard her friend call her by name: "Guadalupe,"[9] she said. Guadalupe. The name of the beautiful angel was Guadalupe.

9 Guadalupe: / gwad - uh - loo - pay /; a woman's name

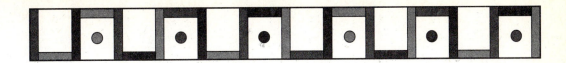

Understanding the Text

What did you understand?

Think about Chapter Six. Find the correct answer to each question. Write the correct letter on the line next to the number.

1. _____ What grade was Javier placed in?
2. _____ How did Javier's teacher speak?
3. _____ How much English did Javier understand?
4. _____ Javier had trouble listening to his teacher. What was he daydreaming about?
5. _____ What did Javier see on the walls of his classroom?
6. _____ Where did Javier's classmates come from?
7. _____ What was Guadalupe doing when Javier first saw her?
8. _____ How did Javier feel when Guadalupe looked at him?

a. writing

b. embarrassed

c. not one word

d. very fast

e. Asia & other places

f. eleventh

g. fighting chickens

h. colorful posters

Interpreting the Text

*What **else** did you understand?*

Use information in Chapter Six to answer these questions. Discuss your answers with your classmates. Show your classmates the paragraphs which helped you answer the questions.

1. Javier thought *"he was having a vision."* What did he mean?

_____

_____

2. Why did Javier think about chickens?

_____

_____

3. How can you describe Javier's classmates?

_____

_____

4. What kind of a student is Guadalupe?

_____

_____

5. Will Guadalupe like Javier? Why? Why not?

_____

_____

6. How will Guadalupe help Javier?

_____

_____

7. Will Javier be a successful student? Why? Why not?

_____

_____

Real Life Skills

Planning Ahead

1. What attracted Javier to Guadalupe?

_____

_____

2. What are the five most important qualities for your own ideal mate (husband, wife, girlfriend, boyfriend)? Make a list.

   a.   c.   e.

   b.   d.

3. Compare your list with a classmate. Share your answers with the whole class. Vote on the five most important qualities for a mate.

Building Your Vocabulary

Shapes

Javier said that Guadalupe's eyes were oval. What shape is *oval*? Write the word "oval" under the correct shape.

Match the words below with the shapes to the left. Write the correct word under the correct shape.

rectangle
circle
triangle
square
cube
horizontal line
vertical line
cone
half circle
   (semi-circle)
oval

Look around your classroom. What shapes do you see? List the objects that have these shapes:

rectangle _____   circle _____

_____   _____

triangle _____   square _____

_____   _____

cube _____   cone _____

_____   _____

oval _____   vertical line _____

_____   _____

horizontal line _____   semi-circle _____

_____   _____

Real Life Skills

Giving Directions

Take out a piece of paper and pencil. Draw a large circle in the center of the paper. In the middle of the circle, draw a short vertical line. Below the vertical line, draw a half circle. Now put a small oval to the left of the vertical line, but still inside the circle. Put another small oval to the right of the vertical line, again inside the circle. Just above each oval, draw a short horizontal line. Now draw a triangle above the large circle; the triangle should touch the edge of the circle. Look at your drawing. What do you see? Can you improve this drawing with any other shapes?

Now draw a "creative" picture with at least five shapes. Then give a classmate directions to draw the same picture. Don't show your picture to your classmate. Just use words to describe it. How good were your directions?

Thinking About Geography

In Javier's school, there are students from many countries. There are students from all over the world. Find the names of countries here and circle them. The country names are listed vertically and horizontally. (There are 41 countries included in this puzzle.)

```
N F R A N C E M E X I C O A R I
I I K B P A G G N C S H V U O N
C R U R E N Y H G H R I I S M D
A A W A R A P I L I A N E T A I
R N A Z U D T J A L E A T R N A
A I I I J A P A N E L N N A I P
G R T L L A O S D K L M A L A A
U A K O R E A I T A L Y M I O K
A Q P O L A N D S P A I N A P I
A H O N D U R A S T U R K E Y S
B D E F G U A T E M A L A Q G T
C P A N A M A T A I W A N R E A
C O L O M B I A N O R W A Y R N
S W E D E N T H A I L A N D M S
A R G E N T I N A W X Y Z A A T
R U S S I A N E P A L S U D A N
Z A I R E C O S T A R I C A Y V
```

What country were you born in? _____

7 Lunchtime

Look at the title of this chapter and the illustration.

- ◆ **Where is Javier now?**
- ◆ **Who is he talking to?**
- ◆ **What are the other students doing there?**
- ◆ **What do you think will happen to Javier at lunchtime?**

Thinking About the Past

Answer these questions and then discuss your answers with a classmate.

1. Do you remember your first school lunch in the United States?

_____

_____

2. What school were you attending?

_____

_____

3. What did you eat for lunch? Did you bring your lunch from home? Or did you get lunch in the school cafeteria?

_____

_____

4. Who did you eat lunch with? Did you eat lunch alone or with new friends?

_____

_____

5. What was your impression of the school cafeteria? Can you compare it to a school cafeteria in your native country?

_____

_____

6. How often do you eat in the school cafeteria now?

_____

_____

7. How often do you go home to eat lunch now? Who prepares your lunch for you at home?

_____

_____

Careful reading: Read Chapter Seven carefully.

Lunchtime

1   It was time for lunch. Javier went out onto the school yard. He looked for his sister, Ana, but he didn't see her. So he went into the school cafeteria to buy his lunch. He didn't have a lot of money. He wasn't sure if he had enough money to pay for his lunch. He noticed other students giving the cashier tickets, not money. He didn't have a ticket and he didn't know how to get one. As he stood in line wondering, he looked up and saw Guadalupe and her friend. They were walking toward him.

2   "They're coming to talk to me," Javier thought to himself. "Beautiful Guadalupe and her friend are coming to talk to me!" He didn't say anything aloud.

"You're new here, aren't you?" asked Guadalupe, gently. Javier nodded his head.

"Do you have a lunch ticket?" continued Guadalupe.

3   "No, I don't," he replied.

"Well, I have an extra ticket and I can give it to you until you get your lunch tickets."

"You have an extra ticket?" asked Javier. "How did you get an extra ticket?"

4   "I brought my lunch from home today," explained Guadalupe. She gave Javier the ticket. "You can use my ticket to get your lunch today. And after lunch we can show you where to get a ticket form. After you fill out the application and turn it in, the office will give you lunch tickets and you won't have to pay for your lunch."

"Thank you, thank you very much," said Javier in English.

"Do you speak a little English?" asked Guadalupe.

"Only a little," replied Javier. "Is the ticket form in English?"

5   "It's in English and Spanish. I can help you fill out the form. I can help you a lot with English if you'd like. When I came here from Nicaragua, I only spoke Spanish. And now I'm almost bilingual. That means I speak two languages and having two languages is like having two worlds. It was very difficult at first. I had a lot of trouble. I thought I could learn English in a few months, but it took more than two years," explained Guadalupe with a smile.

6   Javier returned her smile. "She is so beautiful. And she's smart, too," he thought with admiration. When he spoke aloud, he said to her in Spanish, "Someday, I hope I will be bilingual, too. You've been very helpful to me. I thank you for all your help."

7   "We try to help new students because we remember our own arrivals in the United States. It is difficult to come to a foreign country. You sometimes have a lot of problems with language, money . . . all kinds of things. "

8   "Oh, excuse me, I forgot to introduce my friend. This is Tagui.**10** She's from Yerevan, in Armenia. She tries to help new students, too. They need so much and there are so many different problems. Tagui and I try to help new arrivals like you whenever we can. It's easier for me to help you because you and I speak Spanish, but Tagui and I help each other practice English. We also help students from other countries, too. We've helped students from lots of places, like Vietnam and Iran, too. I guess everyone who comes here has a few problems."

9   "I feel lucky that I met you both," said Javier.
    "Well, let us know if we can help you again. We'll see you later. We have to go to a meeting," said Guadalupe as she and Tagui began to walk away.

---

10 **Tagui** : / tag-wee /; a woman's name; in Armenian, queen

"You have to go to a meeting?" asked Javier. He thought that they must be very important people.

Guadalupe laughed. "Yes, it's an International Club meeting. Students from countries all over the world get together."

"What do they meet about?" asked Javier curiously.

10 "Oh, we plan all kinds of things. . . like food festivals and carnivals and fashion shows with costumes from different countries. And we talk about many different ideas from other countries. Today we're planning an International Folkdance Day. You're welcome to come to our meetings and check them out." She paused. "Well, we'd better go or we'll be late."

11 "Well thanks, thanks again," said Javier. "For the ticket and everything." He turned and got back into the cafeteria line. "I hope I haven't missed lunch," he thought. "I'm hungry."

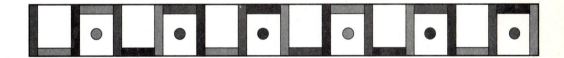

Understanding the Text

What did you understand?

What happened in Chapter Seven? Which event happened (1st)? (2nd)? (3rd)? (4th)? (5th)? Write the correct number in the blank before each sentence.

_____ Guadalupe and Tagui began to walk to the International Club meeting.

_____ Javier went to the cafeteria after looking for his sister.

_____ Guadalupe gave Javier one of her lunch tickets.

_____ Guadalupe introduced Tagui to Javier.

_____ While waiting in line, Guadalupe and a friend talked to Javier.

Think about Chapter Seven. Are the following statements TRUE (T) or FALSE (F)?

_____ 1. Javier wondered if he had enough money to buy lunch.

_____ 2. Guadalupe loaned Javier two lunch tickets.

_____ 3. Guadalupe did not need her lunch ticket today.

_____ 4. Guadalupe is almost bilingual now.

_____ 5. Guadalupe and Tagui helped Javier.

_____ 6. Javier can get lunch tickets from his English teacher.

_____ 7. Javier found his sister, Ana, at lunchtime.

_____ 8. Javier spoke to Guadalupe in English and Spanish.

_____ 9. Tagui is from Iran.

_____10. Javier went to the International Club meeting with Guadalupe and Tagui.

Interpreting the Text

*What **else** did you understand?*

1. **a.** Guadalupe said, "Now I'm almost bilingual." What did she mean?

   _____

   _____

   b. Is anyone in your family bilingual? Who?

   _____

   _____

2. **a.** Guadalupe said, "Having two languages is like having two worlds." What did she mean?

   _____

   _____

b. What are the *benefits* of having two languages?

_____

_____

3. **a.** Guadalupe said, "I thought I could learn English in a few months but it took more than two years." Why did it take Guadalupe more than two years to feel comfortable in English?

_____

_____

b. What can you do to learn English faster?

in the classroom	outside the classroom
do my homework	*listen to English radio*

4. **a.** Guadalupe and Tagui try to help new students at their school. How do you think they help?

_____

_____

b. How can you help new students at your school?

_____

_____

Building Your Vocabulary

Phrasal Verbs

Complete this paragraph. Check the paragraph in parentheses to find the correct word.

Javier went (**1**) _____ onto the school yard at lunchtime. He looked (**1**) _____ his sister, but didn't see her. Before getting in line for lunch, he checked to see if he had enough money. He wasn't sure if he had enough money to pay (**1**) _____ his lunch. At that moment, Guadalupe and her friend Tagui came up to Javier. They came to talk (**2**) _____ him. Guadalupe gave Javier a lunch ticket and told him to fill (**4**) _____ an application for lunch tickets at the office. Later, Guadalupe and Tagui invited Javier to come to International Club meetings. They told him to come and check them (**10**) _____.

Complete the following questions with the correct words. Then interview one of your classmates. Write down your classmate's answers.

go out	pay for	talk to	check out
look for	look up	fill out	

1. Do you _____ on the weekends? Where do you go?

2. How much did you _____ your notebook? Where did you buy it?

3. Did you have to _____ a form for lunch tickets at our school?

4. Who do you normally _____ on the phone?

5. Did you _____ the clubs at school?

6. Do you ever _____ at the sky to see the stars at night?

7. When I _____ a new pair of jeans, where should I go?

Real Life Skills

School Clubs

Guadalupe and Tagui are going to an International Club meeting. What has the club organized?

1. *carnivals*
2.
3.
4.

Does your school have clubs? Fill in this chart with correct information.

Club names	Meeting times and places

Does your school have an International Club? If so, when does it meet? If not, what kind of club does your school need? What are some activities you could plan?

Club	Activities

With other club members, Guadalupe and Tagui are planning many International Club activities at their school. They make posters to advertise the Club events. Look at the International Club announcements below. Complete the posters with the following words:

on

When

in

Monday, March 3

Where

at

to

Free for students/$1 for guests

in the school cafeteria

What time

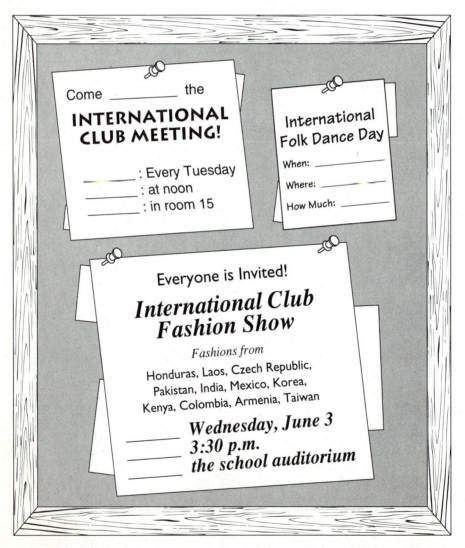

On the Yard

Look at the chapter title and illustration.

- ◆ **Where are Javier and his friends now?**
- ◆ **Is Spider with Javier? How do you know?**
- ◆ **What are they talking about?**
- ◆ **What do you see on this school yard?**
- ◆ **In what ways is this school yard like the yard at your school?**
- ◆ **At your school, when do students go out on the yard?**
- ◆ **What do the students do on the yard at your school?**

Previewing: Scanning for Details

What is Chapter Eight about? **Scan** some of the paragraphs in Chapter Eight to find out some details about the story. Remember to work quickly!

Where is Javier? (paragraph 1) _____

Where is Javier now? (paragraph 2) _____

Who did Javier see on the yard? (paragraph 2) _____

Who did Javier meet on the yard? (paragraphs 3 & 4)_____

What kind of car does Spider have? (paragraph 5)_____

Who does Javier see across the yard? (paragraph 6) _____

Who is Ana's new friend? (paragraph 9) _____

Where are Ana and Javier going now? (paragraph 11)_____

Careful reading: Read Chapter Eight carefully.

On the Yard

1   In the cafeteria, Javier chose two food packages and put them on his tray. He didn't know what was inside the packages. He was too shy to ask anybody. He took a carton of milk and gave his ticket to the cashier. Javier sat down in the cafeteria and ate the food in the packages. The food tasted okay. He liked the spicy burrito and the green jello. After lunch, Javier went outside onto the yard.

2   On the yard, Javier looked for Ana again. He was surprised to see Spider. Spider approached Javier with a big grin.

    "Hey man, how're you doing?" said Spider offering his hand to Javier.

3   "Let me introduce you to some of the guys." Javier looked around and listened as Spider told him the names of his many friends. Javier was happy to meet Chuy[11] because he remembered that in Guadalajara he had a friend whose name was Chuy, too.

4   Spider introduced him to Radislav[12] who was from Bulgaria. And then he met Byung[13] who was Korean. Byung had moved from Korea to Argentina when he was small, so he spoke Spanish and Korean. Radislav spoke a little Spanish, too. Javier was very surprised. As they spoke to him, he noticed that they all spoke Spanish for awhile and then they changed back into English. Then they changed back to Spanish.

5   All of this was very interesting to Javier because he understood a lot of what they were saying. He watched quietly, but did not say very much. Everybody seemed

11 **Chuy:** / choo - ee /; a nickname in Spanish
12 **Radislav:** / rad - is - lav /; a man's name
13 **Byung:** / bee - yung /; a man's name

friendly. Javier began to relax. Radislav was telling him about Spider's car. He told him that Spider had a really nice car. The car was an old car that Spider had fixed up, a Chevrolet. Radislav called it a "Chevy" for short. Radislav said that the Chevy was a real beauty. Javier thought about having a car. Soon he would be able to drive. He was almost old enough now. He just needed experience. With a car, he could go wherever he wanted. He looked at Spider. He thought about Spider's Chevrolet. He was sure that even an old car cost a lot of money. He wondered how Spider had earned enough money for a car.

6   As he was thinking, Javier looked across the yard. His sister, Ana, was waving at him. She had been looking for him.

"Hey, I've got to go, Spider," Javier said. "My little sister's all alone. I'll see you guys later."

"Right, buddy," said Spider. "See you, later."

7   Javier walked across the yard toward Ana. Before Javier could open his mouth, Ana began speaking to him. "Oh, Javier, so many things happened to me this morning. I got lost on the way to my class. A student helped me find my classroom. But I arrived late and the teacher got angry at me. I started to cry and the helpful student put her arm around me so I wouldn't feel bad, but . . . "

8   "Wait a minute, Ana," interrupted Javier, "you're talking so fast that I can't understand anything you're saying. Slow down, slow down."

9   Ana began to laugh. "You're right, Javier. I feel like everything is happening so quickly. I only wanted to tell you that I have a nice new friend. Her name is Celia. She helped me a lot. She told me that the teacher is very nice but doesn't like students to arrive late."

10   "Don't worry, Ana," said Javier. "You won't be late anymore because you won't get lost anymore. You know your way around school now. I'm glad you made a new friend. I met some nice people today, too," Javier said. He was thinking of Spider's friends. He was also thinking of Guadalupe, but he didn't want to tell his sister.

11   The bell rang. "I have much more to tell you, Javier," said Ana. "But I have to hurry to class."

    "Don't be late! I'll see you after school." It was time to go to class.

Understanding the Text

What did you understand?

Think about Chapter Eight. Answer the following questions by circling the correct answer. Indicate the paragraph with the answer.

1. **In the cafeteria, Javier chose _____ food packages.**

   a. two   **c.** four

   b. three

   In which paragraph did you find the answer? _____

2. **Javier took _____ of milk too.**

   a. one carton   **c.** three cartons

   b. two cartons

   In which paragraph did you find the answer? _____

3. **Javier ate _____ jello.**

   a. red   **c.** green

   b. yellow

   In which paragraph did you find the answer? _____

4. **Javier met Spider's friends from _____.**
   a. Bulgaria and Laos   c. Iran and Taiwan
   b. Bulgaria and Korea

   In which paragraph did you find the answer? _____

5. **Byung spoke Korean and Spanish because he had lived in _____ .**
   a. Korea and Venezuela   c. Korea and Argentina
   b. Korea and Nicaragua

   In which paragraph did you find the answer? _____

6. **When Spider's friends spoke together, they spoke _____.**
   a. English only   c. English and Spanish
   b. Spanish only

   In which paragraph did you find the answer? _____

7. **Spider had a _____ Chevrolet.**
   a. new   c. 1983
   b. fixed up

   In which paragraph did you find the answer? _____

8. **Ana had trouble finding _____ the first day of class.**
   a. her classroom   c. the cafeteria
   b. a new friend

   In which paragraph did you find the answer? _____

9. **Ana's teacher got angry because she doesn't like students _____.**
   a. to talk in class   c. to arrive late
   b. to cry

   In which paragraph did you find the answer? _____

Interpreting the Text

*What **else** did you understand?*

1. Do you think Javier likes Spider? Why? Why not?

_____

_____

2. Do you think Spider likes Javier? Why? Why not?

_____

_____

3. Spider has a car. How do you think Spider earned enough money to buy the car?

_____

_____

4. What are some ways to earn money to buy a car?

_____

_____

5. Javier wants a car of his own. Do you think he'll get a car soon? Why? Why not?

_____

_____

6. What are the advantages and disadvantages of having a car?

_____

_____

7. Do you like cars? If so, what kinds of cars do you like? If not, why not?

_____

_____

_____

_____

Building Your Vocabulary

Discovering Familiar Words

Unscramble the words below to discover words describing cafeteria food.

Lunch Menu

zpiza _____

rnoc odgs _____

euhmabrgrs _____

lasads _____

kilm _____

eaorngs _____

tifru _____

tchcoolae limk _____

enroag ujeic _____

eppals _____

iockoes _____

crfenh rfsie _____

toh gsdo _____

cei recam _____

Javier ate a spicy burrito and jello for lunch. What do your classmates like to eat for lunch? Before you interview your classmates, decide on a question you want to ask them. Write the question below.

_____

Classmate's name	Favorite lunch
1.	
2.	
3.	
4.	
5.	
6.	

Real Life Skills

Creating an Ideal Menu for Your School

What would you like your school cafeteria menu to include?
Write your ideal lunch menu below.

Cafeteria Menu

9   Car Love

Look at the title of the chapter and the illustration.

- ◆ **What do you think Javier is interested in?**
- ◆ **How difficult is it to buy a car?**
- ◆ **Do you think Javier will be able to buy a car soon?**

Careful reading: Now read Chapter Nine carefully.

Car Love

1   Javier spent a lot of time during the next few weeks thinking about cars. He thought about getting his driver's license, learning to drive, and buying a car. Spider had shown Javier his beautiful Chevy. Javier was impressed. The Chevy was a nice car. Someday, he promised himself, he would have a car like that.

2   "Did you hear me, Javier?" Javier jumped. He heard the sound of his teacher's voice interrupting his daydreams. "Javier?" she repeated. "Are you daydreaming? I asked you to tell us the capital of California."

3   "Sacramento," Javier said quickly. "And Detroit is the capital of Michigan . . . where they make Fords and Chevys."

Everyone laughed. The teacher, Ms. Silver, laughed too. "No," she said, "Detroit is not the capital of Michigan. And you're daydreaming when you should be paying attention. I'm glad you're interested in cars Javier, but we're working on state capitals now. Stay with us," she advised gently. "Who can raise his hand and tell me the capital of Michigan?"

4   Guadalupe's hand shot up into the air. When Ms. Silver called on Lupe,[14] she said confidently, "Lansing is the capital of Michigan."

"That's correct, Lupe. Very good. But it's also true that Detroit is a big, important city in Michigan and they make a lot of cars there."

5   "I know, Ms. Silver. I have pictures of cars they used to make in Detroit. These are old cars," Javier said, taking out a large stack of photos from a folder. "Aren't they beautiful?"

14 **Lupe:** / loo - pay /; a nickname for Guadalupe

6   Ms. Silver smiled again. She was glad Javier was so interested in cars. She thought it was important for students to have special hobbies. She took a moment from the lesson on state capitals to let Javier show a few of his photos. The class enjoyed looking at the old cars.

7   "Where did you get those pictures?" asked one student.

"There was an auto show downtown. I went with my Dad. They gave us all these photos for free. The show was great."

"Thank you, Javier," said Ms. Silver. "Now, who remembers where these cars were made?"

8   "Detroit, Michigan," a few students answered together.

"And what's the capital of Michigan?" she asked again.

"Lansing," the class replied.

"Right! And the capital of California, Javier?"

"Sacramento," said Javier. He was paying attention now.

"Right again!" said Ms. Silver.

9   The bell rang. Class was over. Guadalupe waited for Javier. Together they walked out to the yard.

"What's up?" said Spider walking toward them. "What's happening, brother?"

"Not too much, Spider," answered Javier.

"Do you need a ride home today? I'm driving right by your place."

10   "I sure do! Wow! A ride would be great! Could you take Lupe, too?"

"Sure, brother, no problem," said Spider.

"Oh, that's okay," said Lupe. "I don't need a ride. Anyway, my folks might get upset."

"Lighten up, Lupe," Javier said, putting his arm around her shoulder. "Your folks won't get upset and I want you to see how Spider's Chevy drives. It's great!"

"All cars are the same to me, Javier," she answered. "I've told you already. It doesn't matter to me what they look like." She took his arm off of her shoulder.

11   "Uh, hey guys, I've got to go. I'll meet you in the parking lot after school." Spider quickly walked away. He didn't like to be around couples when they were uptight.

"Thanks, amigo[15]," said Javier. "See you after school."

"Yeah," answered Spider, "see you."

Javier turned to Guadalupe. She looked upset. "What's the matter, Lupe?" he asked her.

"I don't want to go in Spider's car. My father will get mad at me."

12   "Well, it's okay if you don't want to. I only wanted you to ride home with me. You know I like to be with you."

"I like to be with you, too, Javier. But not with Spider. He's trouble."

"What do you mean, Lupe? He's a good guy."

13   "I know he's nice to you, Javier, but I'm worried. He has those tattoos and I'm not sure if he's in a gang, but I know my father gets mad about stuff like that."

"Like what? Lots of people have tattoos. It doesn't mean they're in gangs."

"I know. But I'm pretty sure Spider *is* in a gang. He hangs out with all the gang guys and he, well, he acts like he's in a gang."

14   "Look, Lupe, why are we fighting? You're my girlfriend and I'm not in a gang. We don't have to worry about Spider, " explained Javier.

"Well, we don't have to worry about him if you don't hang out with him too much."

15 **amigo:** / uh - mee - go /; Spanish for friend

"Let's not talk about it anymore right now. Okay? I'll call you tonight."

"Are you going home in Spider's car?" asked Lupe.

Javier did not look at her. He did not say anything, either.

15   "Well, Javier, aren't you going to answer me?"

"I've got to go. I'll call you tonight." Javier leaned over and kissed Guadalupe on the cheek. She did not look up at him.

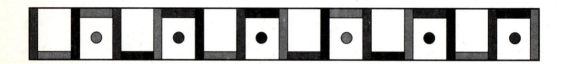

Understanding the Text

What did you understand?

Think about Chapter Nine. Are the following statements TRUE (T) or FALSE (F)? If the statement is false, correct it so that it is true.

_____ 1. At the beginning of class, Javier was paying close attention to his teacher, Ms. Silver.

_____

_____ 2. Ms. Silver was teaching about capital cities of countries around the world.

_____

_____ 3. Javier knew the capital of California.

_____

_____ 4. Javier knew the capital of Michigan.

_____

_____ 5. Javier had only one photo of an antique car.

_____

_____ 6. Javier received free photos when attending an auto show with his father.

_____

_____ 7. Javier wanted to ride home in Spider's car.

_____

_____ 8. Guadalupe is interested in cars.

_____

_____ 9. Guadalupe doesn't like Spider.

_____

_____ 10. Javier told Lupe that he was going home in Spider's car.

_____

Interpreting the Text

What **else** did you understand?

1. What kind of class are Javier and Lupe in together?

_____

_____

2. What kind of student is Lupe?

_____

_____

3. Why is Lupe upset with Javier?

_____

_____

4. Why is Javier upset with Lupe?

_____

_____

5. Lupe thinks Spider is in a gang. Do you think he is in a gang? Why? Why not?

_____

_____

6. Spider offered to give Javier a ride home in his car. Do you think Javier will go home in Spider's car after school? Why? Why not?

_____

_____

7. Lupe's parents will get upset if she goes home with Spider. Why?

_____

_____

8. Would your family get upset if you had a friend like Spider? Why? Why not?

_____

_____

Building Your Vocabulary

Phrasal Verbs

Read these sentences and then answer the questions.

1. Javier is *interested in* cars. What are you interested in?

_____

_____

2. Javier *daydreams about* cars. What do you daydream about?

_____

_____

3. Javier *was impressed with* Spider's car. What are you impressed with?

_____

_____

4. Spider *hangs out with* "gang guys." Who do you hang out with?

_____

_____

5. Lupe's parents *get upset about* boys with tattoos. What does your family get upset about?

_____

_____

6. Javier is *thinking about* getting his driver's license. What are you thinking about?

_____

_____

Interview a classmate. Ask the following questions. Write down all answers using your classmate's name.

1. What are you *interested in*?

_____

2. What do you *daydream about*?

_____

3. What *are* you *impressed with*?

_____

4. Who do you *hang out with*?

_____

5. What do you *get upset about*?

_____

6. Are you *thinking about* getting a driver's license?

_____

Real Life Skills

Getting a Car

What is Javier thinking about doing? Look in paragraph 1 and complete this short paragraph with the correct words.

Javier is daydreaming in class. He isn't really paying attention to his teacher, Ms. Silver. He is thinking about getting his _____, learning to _____, and buying _____.

What do *you* need to get a driver's license?

1.   2.   3.

What do *you* need to do to learn to drive?

1.   2.   3.

What do *you* need to do to buy a car?

1.   2.   3.

Thinking About Geography

Javier's classmates are learning about states and capitals. Circle the 50 states of the United States of America and Washington, D. C. in this word puzzle. Words are listed horizontally (from left to right) and vertically (from top to bottom).

```
A R I Z O N A * J C H L M M H N N R P Q P W T S
L * C O L O R A D O A O I I K E O O H E R W E O P
A U T A H * K K E N W U N S N W R R O N J A S R C
B B C I O W A A L N A I N S L * T T D N K S T B A
A E F G Q P N N A E I S E I O J H H E S E H * Z L
M H C * O S S S W C I I S S N E * * * Y F I V S I
A L A S K A A A A T L A O S E R C D I L G N I R F
* X L A Z U S S R I L N T I W S A A S V H G R E O
Y J I D A H O * E C I A A P * E R K L A I T G L R
I K F L O R I D A U N C D P H Y O O A N O O I B N
G E O R G I A * V T O I H I A F L T N I N N P I
* D A U O P L * P E I Y R Q M P I A D A * P I O A
T M O N T A N A A B S J K D P G N S S A Q C A B *
E I N D I A N A * F * G B H S N A O V E R M O N T
X M I K L I O H I O * J I O H E S U V T J I N G W
A N A R * N M I C H I G A N I V O T I T L U E R I
S O P Q K E N T U C K Y * N R A R H R A Z * W S S
M A R Y L A N D O R E G O N E D E * G C D T * N C
M A S S A C H U S E T T S B * A G D I B A W M V O
N E B R A S K A M I S S O U R I O A N C P U E X N
N E W * Y O R K O K L A H O M A N K I D R V X Q S
S O U T H * C A R O L I N A C F * O A S X E I A I
T E N N E S S E E T W Y O M I N G T Y Z T W C * N
W A S H I N G T O N * D * C L M M A I N E * O A V
```

What state do you live in? _____

What is the capital of your state? _____

Building Your Vocabulary

Antonyms

Words that have **opposite** meanings are called **antonyms**. Fill in the crossword puzzle with the antonyms of the words below. You can find the antonyms in Chapter Nine. Read the paragraph in parentheses to find the antonym.

Across

1 down (paragraph 4)
3 false (paragraph 4)
5 relaxed (paragraph 11)
6 forgets (paragraph 7)
8 small (paragraph 5)

Down

1 happy (paragraph 10)
2 cried (paragraph 3)
3 away (paragraph 9)
4 selling (paragraph 1)
7 new (paragraph 5)

Abuelita's Visit

Look at the title of the chapter and the illustration.

- ◆ **What do you remember about Javier's grandmother?**
- ◆ **Why do you think Javier's grandmother has come to the U.S.?**
- ◆ **How has Javier changed since he last saw his grandmother?**

Careful reading: Now read Chapter Ten carefully.

Abuelita's Visit

1   After school, Javier went home in Spider's Chevy. As they drove, they talked about the car. Spider had fixed the transmission himself and painted the car "Candy Apple Red." Many of his friends had helped Spider work on the car. It was an old car and sometimes needed car parts replaced. But now, Spider was worried. The car was running fine and it looked fine, but he didn't have enough money to take care of it. He didn't have any money and he had lost his part-time job.

2   "I didn't know you had a part-time job, Spider," said Javier.

"Well, I don't anymore. They laid me off and now I don't have any money. I was thinking of selling my car. Or maybe I'll quit school and try to get a full-time job. I owe my brother some money and he needs it."

"I guess everyone has problems. I was thinking you didn't have any problems. You know, you've got this great car, you have so many friends, and well, you really know the ropes."

3   Spider laughed. "Javier, my brother, you are too funny for words! I have so many problems with school, with my family, no job, no money, and the gang problems. Hey, I don't want to talk about all this stuff. It's a downer!"

"Gee, I wish I could help you in some way, Spider," said Javier. "I sometimes think about dropping out of school. I need money, too. But Lupe said she'd break up with me if I dropped out. She says if you want to be somebody someday, you have to finish school. I don't know."

4   "Hey, everybody's got problems. We all have to face our problems. You've got yours, I've got mine. We do the best we can. Don't worry about it, my friend. You help me every time I see your smiling face." They drove along in silence for awhile. They were thinking about their problems.

Javier looked up. They had arrived at his house. "Well, here we are, at your house," said Spider. Javier picked up his stuff and opened the car door.

"Thanks for the ride, Spider. Your car is great!"

"Yeah, yeah," smiled Spider. "I know."

5   Javier shut the car door and went inside. When he went into the kitchen, he was surprised to see his grandmother sitting at the table. With her long, thin fingers and her strong face, Abuelita looked calm and beautiful. She was not a young woman, but Javier did not see her age.

"Abuelita," he said to her. "Abuelita, it's so good to see you." He went over and gave her a hug. Javier had missed his grandmother.

"How are you, Abuelita?" asked Javier. "I'm so happy you're here with us."

6   "I'm fine, Javier. I'm glad to see that you are growing. You look big and tall. Your father and mother tell me you eat a lot of food these days. That's good. And you go to school everyday. That's good, too. And what else?"

"Oh, many things, Abuelita. I have so many things to tell you."

"Are you learning English?" asked Abuelita.

"Yes, a little. I can say many things now. But there are also many other things I cannot say or write. English is very difficult."

"Of course it is. It takes people many years to learn English. And some people never learn; they give up. Do you have a good teacher?"

7   "Yes, I have many good teachers. And I have a girlfriend, a novia.**16** She is very beautiful, like an angel. Her name is Lupe. She speaks English very well and she helps me with my English."

8   "I hope I will get to meet this Guadalupe angel. And I hope your English will improve. Now tell me about your other friends. Your sister, Ana, tells me you have two friends with very strange names. One is Spider and the other is, hmmm, let me see . . . Raslof, is that correct?"

9   "Spider and Radislav. Spider is from El Salvador and Radislav is from Bulgaria. Spider has a beautiful old Chevrolet. He wants to sell it and I'm going to try to buy it. I don't know how, but I'm going to try to figure it out."

10   "It sounds like many things have changed for you, Javier. You are growing up. Girlfriends and cars and money are nice things to have, but don't forget the important things you and I have always talked about. Don't forget to be good inside, Javier."

11   "Now you are talking like Lupe, Abuela. She doesn't like cars very much. And she doesn't like Spider, either. She says other things are more important, like being a good, decent person."

12   "She seems like a very strong girl, Javier. I like strong females. Now I am sure I want to meet her. But, tell me, Javier, why doesn't Guadalupe like your friend, Spider? Does she like Radislav?"

"She likes Radislav because he doesn't have a tattoo or drive a Chevy. She thinks Spider is in a gang."

16 novia: / no - vee - uh /; Spanish for girlfriend

"And is he in a gang? A pandilla?"[17] asked Abuelita.

13   Javier was surprised. He thought that his grandmother didn't know anything about gangs, but he was wrong.

"I think so, Abuelita. Do you know about gangs?"

"Yes, I know about gangs. Everyone has heard about gangs. It is important to know what is true about gangs and what isn't true. It's also important to find out if Spider is in a gang. Because if he is, he may be in trouble and need help. If you're his friend, you may have to help him."

14   "I'll find out. I'll find out if he's in a gang. I know he has a lot of problems, but he doesn't like to talk about them."

"Nobody likes to talk about their problems, Javier.

15 But that's what friends are for, to help other friends with problems."

16   "I'm so glad you're here, Abuelita. I've missed talking to you. You're so wise. You really know a lot of important things about life."

"I'm not very wise, but I have lived for a long time. And I plan to keep living awhile longer," Abuelita said with a laugh.

"That's good," said Javier. "Now I'm going to call Lupe and tell her you're here. But I'm not going to tell her that I have a plan to buy Spider's car."

"You keep secrets from her, already?" asked Abuelita with a smile.

Javier smiled back at his grandmother.

17 pandilla: / pan - dee - ya /; Spanish for gang

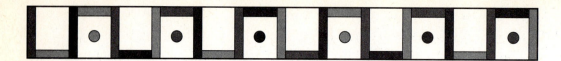

Understanding the Text

What did you understand?

Think about Chapter Ten. Are these statements TRUE (T) or FALSE (F)? If the statement is false, correct it.

_____ 1. Javier went home from school in Spider's "Sky Blue" Chevy.

_____

_____ 2. Spider's car was in poor condition because he didn't have enough money to fix it.

_____

_____ 3. Spider lost his full-time job.

_____

_____ 4. Spider's brother owes him money.

_____

_____ 5. Javier wants to help Spider solve his problems.

_____

_____ 6. Javier was surprised to see his grandmother when he arrived home.

_____

_____ 7. Javier's grandmother wants to meet Spider and Radislav.

_____

_____ 8. Javier is in a gang.

_____

_____ 9. Abuelita thinks Javier needs to help Spider.

_____

_____ 10. Javier is keeping a secret from Lupe.

_____

Interpreting the Text

*What **else** did you understand?*

1. Spider lost his part-time job. Why did Spider get laid off from his job?

_____

_____

2. Spider has been friendly to Javier. Why is Spider so nice to Javier?

_____

_____

3. Spider has many problems. Will Javier have the same problems as Spider in the future? Why? Why not?

_____

_____

4. What can Javier learn from his grandmother?

_____

_____

5. In what ways are Abuelita and Lupe similar?

_____

_____

6. Why does Spider owe his brother money?

_____

_____

7. Lupe says it's important to be a good decent person. What do *you* think is important?

_____

_____

Real Life Skills

Solving Problems

Look at section 3 in this chapter and fill in this statement:

Spider said, "I have so many _____ with school, with

my _____, no _____, _____ money,

and the gang problems."

What kinds of problems does Spider have?

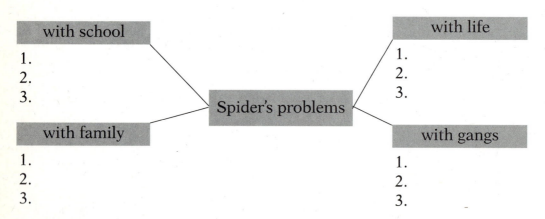

Abuelita said that Spider "may be in trouble and need help. If you're his friend, you may have to help him." How can Javier help Spider?

Building Your Vocabulary

Descriptive Adjectives

Javier's grandmother was old but "Javier did not see her age." What did he see? Can you describe Javier's grandmother?

Circle the words below that describe Javier's grandmother. Use the descriptive adjectives in your answers to the questions below.

kind	calm	nice	short
thin	mean	elegant	old
impatient	beautiful	nervous	considerate
patient	pretty	thoughtful	attractive
experienced	worldly	young	gentle
tall	helpful	wise	inconsiderate

What kind of personality does Javier's grandmother have?

_____

_____

_____

What does Javier's grandmother look like?

_____

_____

_____

Who is your favorite old person? Describe that person. Think about these questions when you write your description:

◆ What is your favorite old person's name?
◆ Where is he/she from?
◆ What is your relation to him/her?
◆ What does he/she look like?
◆ What do you like about your favorite person?
◆ Why is he/she your favorite old person?

My favorite old person is _____

_____

_____

_____

Building Your Vocabulary

Phrasal Verbs

Complete each sentence with one of the phrasal verbs listed below. Use each phrasal verb only once. Use the correct tense.

drop out of	grown up	talk about
lay off	figure out	find out
give up	break up with	pick up

1. Spider was _____ from his job.

2. Javier and Lupe often _____ the future.

3. Lupe might _____ Javier if he doesn't finish school.

4. Lupe doesn't want Javier to _____ school.

5. Javier doesn't want to _____ studying English.

6. Javier wants to _____ his math homework.

7. Spider _____ Javier in the school parking lot.

8. Javier has _____ since he saw his grandmother.

9. Javier wants to _____ if Spider is in a gang.

Complete the following sentences with the correct word. You can find the correct word in the section of the chapter in parentheses. Answer the questions that follow.

Example:

Spider was laid __*off*__ from his part-time job. (2)

Do you know anyone who has been laid __*off*__ from a job?

  Yes, my brother was laid off from his job.

1. Spider's friends helped him work ____ his Chevy.   (1)

   Have you ever worked ____ a car?

   _____

2. Spider didn't have enough money to take care ____ his car.   (1)

   Do you have enough money to take care ____ a car?

   _____

3. Javier wants to buy Spider's car. He is going to try to figure ____ how to buy it.   (9)

   Have you figured ____ how to save money?

   _____

4. Abuelita thinks that Javier has grown ____ since she saw him in Mexico.   (10)

   Have you grown ____ a lot since you saw one of your grandparents?

   _____

Thinking About the Future

Let's Predict

What do you think is going to happen to Javier in the future? Look at the Table of Contents on page v. Before reading Chapter 11, write your own version of the story below. Try to include Lupe, Spider, and Abuelita in your story.

Javier is happy that his grandmother is visiting his family. He wants her to meet Lupe and Spider. He also wants her to see Spider's car. He hopes that he can buy Spider's car someday.

_____

_____

_____

_____

_____

_____

_____

_____

_____

_____

_____

_____

_____

_____

_____

_____

_____

_____

A Surprise

Read the title of this chapter and look at the illustration.

- ◆ **Where are Lupe and Javier now?**
- ◆ **Javier has a new hobby. What is it?**
- ◆ **Javier has a surprise for Lupe. What do you think it is?**
- ◆ **What do you think is going to happen in Chapter Eleven?**

Careful reading: Now read Chapter Eleven carefully.

A Surprise

1   Time passed. Javier got a job at a local supermarket. He was working as a box boy. He liked his job because he was earning good money. Sometimes he helped people carry groceries to their cars. Sometimes they gave him tips. The job wasn't difficult and it gave Javier many chances to practice his English. As he helped the customers to their cars, he often practiced English with the English speaking customers.

2   Javier worked after school four days a week. Once in awhile, Lupe came to visit him at the supermarket. She was happy he was working. She sometimes waited for him to get off work and then they walked home together. As they walked, they planned their future.

3   "You know, Lupe," said Javier, "pretty soon I'm going to be able to drive you home. I'll have a beautiful Chevy and we'll drive everywhere."

"Javier, I don't mind walking," said Lupe. "I like to walk. When we walk, everything is slower and I like that. This city moves too fast for me. Besides, you won't have enough money to buy a car for a long time."

4   "You're wrong, Lupita. You know I'm saving my salary and my tips, but I'm also working on a special surprise."

"What is it, Javier? Are you keeping a secret from me?"

"Well, yes. I have a little surprise in the works. Come over to my house for a few minutes and I'll show you."

"Okay, Javier," answered Guadalupe. "But I'd better call my mother and tell her where I am."

5   "She knows you're with me, your novio," [18] he smiled. "But you can call her from my house. I want you to see what I'm doing, okay?"

18 **novio:** / no - vee -o /; Spanish for boyfriend

"Okay, Javier. Besides, I want to see your grandmother, your Abuelita again. It's always fun talking with her."

6   They walked more quickly to Javier's house. When they arrived, Abuelita greeted Javier and Guadalupe. She was glad to see Guadalupe again. Abuelita thought that Javier had a lovely girlfriend.

"Good afternoon, Abuelita," said Javier and Guadalupe.

"Abuela, don't tell her about the surprise! I want to show her myself." Javier went out of the room. When he returned, he was carrying a small wooden box. It had a rose carved into the top.

7   "That's a very pretty box, Javier," said Guadalupe.

"I think so, too," said Abuelita. "Javier made it. His father is teaching him how to make boxes and how to carve flowers into them."

Guadalupe was surprised. "You made this box, Javier? And you carved the rose?"

8   Javier felt shy. "It wasn't difficult, Lupe. I've made three boxes already. It doesn't take me very long and I enjoy doing it. It's really fun. When I started, my father helped me. He showed me how to do it and we worked together. Now I can do it by myself. I listen to music and work with my knife." He brought the other two boxes to show her.

"They're so pretty, Javier," said Guadalupe.

"And one of them is for you, Guadalupe," said Javier.

9   "Really? Which one?" asked Guadalupe.

"Choose whichever one you want," said Javier.

Now Guadalupe felt shy. She didn't know which box to choose. They were all different and all pretty. She liked each one. She was happy Javier had made one for her. She was also happy that he was learning to carve. Carving was a fine craft, she thought. "Thank you, Javier. I think I'd like the box with the rose carved on top."

10   "I'm glad you chose that one. I thought you would like it the best," said Javier.

"But I like them all, Javier," said Guadalupe.

"I'm going to sell the other wooden boxes at the swap meet. Then I'll have more money to buy my car. I'm going to try to make enough boxes by Sunday to really earn some money."

11   "You know," Guadalupe said, "I need to think of a way to help you with those lovely boxes. Maybe I can paint designs on the outside of the ones you don't carve. I'll have to practice."

12   "That's a very good idea," said Abuelita, "then you two could work on the boxes together. You might even work while you're at the swap meet selling the boxes. When it isn't crowded with customers, you could paint boxes. By the way, I'd like to go to this swap meet, too. When is it?"

13   "Oh, there's a swap meet twice a month, on Sundays. People sell whatever they have: new things, old things, antiques, junk, whatever. They have it in the parking lot of the college, over there," explained Javier.

14   "I go with my mother every month," said Guadalupe. Then, all of a sudden, she remembered something important. "Oh no! I forgot to call my mother. I'd better hurry home. She'll be worried about me. I hope she won't be angry."

15   Guadalupe picked up her special wooden box and went out the door. "Good-bye everybody," she called. "Good-bye, Abuelita, good-bye, Javier."

"Good-bye, Lupe," they called after her.

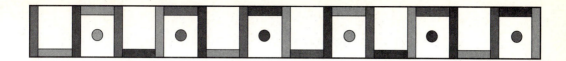

Understanding the Text

What did you understand?

Think about Chapter Eleven. Are the following statements
TRUE (T) or FALSE (F)? If the statement is false, correct it.

_____ 1. Javier works at a movie theater.

_____

_____ 2. Javier parks cars in a parking lot.

_____

_____ 3. Javier works four days a week after school.

_____

_____ 4. Javier hopes to buy a car soon.

_____

_____ 5. Lupe prefers walking to driving a car.

_____

_____ 6. Javier needs his father's help to carve boxes.

_____

_____ 7. Javier carved three wooden boxes for Lupe.

_____

_____ 8. Lupe chose a box with a carved bird.

_____

_____ 9. Javier wants to sell his wooden boxes at an art gallery.

_____

_____ 10. Lupe is going to sell jewelry at the local swap meet.

_____

_____ 11. The swap meet takes place twice a month on Saturdays.

_____

_____ 12. Lupe remembered to call her mother.

_____

Scanning for Details

Scan the chapter for information to complete these exercises. Remember to work quickly.

1. **Javier likes his job. Why? List three reasons.**

   a.   **c.**

   b.

   In which paragraph did you find the answer? _____

2. **Javier likes to carve boxes. Why? List two reasons.**

   a.   **b.**

   In which paragraph did you find the answer? _____

3. **What kinds of things do people sell at the swap meet? List four things.**

   a.   **c.**

   b.   **d.**

   In which paragraph did you find the answer? _____

Interpreting the Text

*What **else** did you understand?*

1. When Lupe and Javier walk home from the supermarket together, they discuss their future.

    a. What do you think they talk about?

    _____

    _____

    b. Do you think they'll break up soon? Why? Why not?

    _____

    _____

    c. Do you think they will still be together in five years? Why? Why not?

    _____

    _____

2. Lupe said that she wanted to see Abuelita again.

    a. What does Lupe like about Javier's grandmother?

    _____

    _____

    b. What does Javier's grandmother like about Lupe?

    _____

    _____

3. Javier hopes to earn enough money to buy a car.

    a. Do you think he can earn enough money by working at the supermarket?

    _____

    _____

    b. Do you think selling carved boxes will help him save money?

    _____

    _____

4. Lupe is happy that Javier is working at the supermarket.

    a. Why is she happy that Javier is working?

    _____

    _____

    b. Do you think Lupe should get a job? Why? Why not?

    _____

    _____

Building Your Vocabulary

Word Groups

People sell a lot of different things at swap meets. Can you add anything to this list?

clothing	tires	toys
pots and pans	silverware	CDs
transistor radios	televisions	used stereos
pants	vests	cassette tapes
flower vases	carved boxes	art
candlesticks	vacuum cleaners	boots
pens and pencils	clocks	dishes
plants and flower pots	coffee mugs and glasses	strollers
games	notebooks	used magazines
books	radiators	hub caps
hangers	pottery	mirrors
antiques	furniture	jeans
raincoats	blouses	skirts
refrigerators	desks	BBQ grills
lawn mowers	lamps	sofas
jewelry	tools	shoes

_____	_____	_____
_____	_____	_____
_____	_____	_____
_____	_____	_____
_____	_____	_____

Can you put the words listed above into categories? Write them on the next page.

What can you buy at a swap meet?

For the kitchen	For the car	For children

Music	For school	Clothing

For the living room	Reading material	For the yard

Miscellaneous		

Real Life Skills

Advertising

Javier and Lupe want to sell carved and painted boxes at the swap meet. What kind of sign can Javier and Guadalupe make to attract customers? Design a sign for them below.

12 A Gang Problem

Read the title of the chapter and look at the illustration.

- ◆ **Who do you see in this illustration?**
- ◆ **What are Abuelita and Javier doing?**
- ◆ **How do Javier's parents and sister feel?**
- ◆ **What do you think is going to happen in Chapter Twelve?**

Careful reading: Now read Chapter Twelve carefully.

A Gang Problem

1   The swap meet was great! Javier sold all the boxes he had carved. Lupe also painted one of the boxes in the morning and sold it in the afternoon. They enjoyed taking turns walking around and looking at all the different things people were selling. Abuelita was with them. She enjoyed walking around and seeing what was for sale. They all liked bargaining for good prices at the swap meet. Abuelita spent a little money and Javier earned some money, so everyone had a good time.

    Javier and Lupe had to pack up their display tables and go home in the late afternoon. On the way home, Javier and his grandmother dropped Lupe off at her house. Then, they went home. Javier parked his father's car and began to unload the display tables. His mother came out of the house.

2   "Javier," she called. "Spider is on the phone. It's the third time he's called you in the last fifteen minutes. It sounds like he really needs to speak to you."

3   Javier got a strange feeling in his stomach. As he ran to talk to Spider, his mind was racing. He knew that if Spider had called three times in fifteen minutes, there was a problem. He knew Spider was having problems. He was worried. He quickly picked up the phone and tried to sound calm.

    "Hey, Spider, what's up?" asked Javier.

    For a short second, there was silence at the other end of the line. Then, Spider spoke. "Javier, my friend, listen to me. You've got to listen to me."

    "Hey, Spider, what's wrong? You sound bad. You sound terrible. What's going on?" asked Javier, still trying to sound calm.

4   "It's bad. It's my brother. One of the other gangs drove by our house. My brother was outside waxing his car. They shot him. I don't know why, but they shot him. I know they're going to come back. I need your help."

"You've got it. What do you need, my friend?" asked Javier.

"I need you to drive me over to their place. In *my* car. I just want to talk to them," said Spider.

5   Javier had a strange feeling in his stomach again. He knew that there was going to be trouble. "I'll be over there right away, Spider," Javier said in a quiet, low voice.

"No, I'll come pick you up," said Spider. "Right now, okay?"

"Right," agreed Javier.

6   When he hung up the telephone, he tried to appear calm. He did not want to worry his family. But everyone knew that if Spider was calling, there was a problem. A gang problem. When Javier turned around, his father, his mother, his sister, and his grandmother were all standing, waiting to hear what had happened.

"I need to help Spider," explained Javier. "I'm going to drive him to his friend's house."

"What for? Why does he need you to drive him, Javier? Why can't he drive himself? What's going on?" asked Mr. Flores.

"Well, I don't exactly know, but I'm going to drive his car. He asked me to drive it for him," said Javier.

"Is he going with you?" asked Mr. Flores.

"Yes," said Javier.

7   "Why can't he drive himself?" asked Mr. Flores in a worried voice. "You don't need to drive him anywhere. I don't want you to get into any trouble. Spider is probably having trouble with a gang and that is none of our business."

"Your father is right, Javier. We don't want any trouble," added Mrs. Flores.

8   "Just a minute, here," interrupted Abuelita. "Javier is trying to be a good friend. Maybe his friend Spider *is* in a gang and having a gang problem. If this is true, then we have to help him. That's what friends are for. Come on, Javier, let's go."

Javier and his grandmother started to leave.

9   "You can't go with him, Abuelita. This could be very dangerous," said Mr. Flores.

"That's exactly why I must go. When there is danger, we must all be brave and stick together. That's what makes a strong family. Now let's hurry, Javier."

10   Javier and his grandmother quickly ran outside. They saw the red Chevy coming up the street. Spider was driving fast. He screeched to a stop. Javier and his grandmother started to get in the car.

"Wait a minute, man," said Spider. "What's your Abuelita doing?" Spider looked pale and frightened.

"She's coming with us. She knows a lot about gangs and gang problems. It's okay, Spider. Believe me."

11   Spider didn't say anything. He wasn't feeling too good. Abuelita got in the back seat. Spider moved over to the passenger seat. "You're driving, right?" he asked Javier. Javier got in behind the wheel.

12   "Right. I'm driving." Javier looked up and saw his family looking out of the house. They looked very worried as they watched Spider's Chevy drive away.

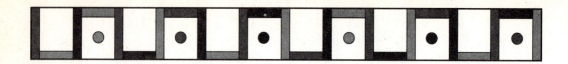

Understanding the Text

What did you understand?

Think about Chapter Twelve. What happened first (1st)? second (2nd)? third (3rd)? fourth (4th)? fifth (5th)? sixth (6th)? seventh (7th)? eighth (8th)? ninth (9th)?

_____ Javier, Lupe, and Abuelita spent most of the day at the swap meet.

_____ Spider called Javier on the phone a few times.

_____ Javier's mother, father, and sister were unhappy when Javier decided to help Spider.

_____ Before returning home, Javier and Abuelita dropped Lupe off at her home.

_____ Javier talked to Spider on the telephone.

_____ Spider asked Javier to do him a favor.

_____ Javier and Abuelita got into Spider's car and drove off.

_____ Spider told Javier that his brother was shot in a gang shooting.

_____ Javier agreed to drive Spider to another neighborhood.

Interpreting the Text

*What **else** did you understand?*

Prove that these statements are true with information from the chapter. Write the information below the statement. Follow the example:

Javier drove his father's car to the swap meet.

   Javier parked his father's car.

1. Abuelita bought something at the swap meet.

---

2. Javier and Lupe walked around the swap meet individually.

_____

3. Spider was anxious to speak with Javier.

_____

4. Javier was worried about Spider.

_____

5. Spider was nervous.

_____

6. Javier's parents were unhappy with Javier's decision.

_____

What Do You Think?

Answer these questions. Use your own ideas. The answers are not in the chapter.

1. Spider was in trouble and Javier decided to help him out. Do you think Javier made the right decision?

_____

_____

2. Abuelita decided to go with Javier. Did she make the right decision?

_____

_____

3. What would you do in a similar situation?

_____

_____

Thinking About the Future

Let's Predict

Look at the Table of Contents on page v. What do you think is going to happen to Javier, Abuelita, Spider, and Lupe in the next two chapters?

Example: Ana *is worried about her brother and Spider. She is going to try to help them.*

Javier _____

_____

_____

Abuelita _____

_____

_____

Spider _____

_____

_____

Lupe _____

_____

_____

Building Your Vocabulary

Descriptive Adjectives

Read the following statements and then answer the questions.

1. Spider sounded *terrible* on the phone. Why?

_____

_____

2. After speaking with Spider on the phone, Javier tried to appear *calm*. Was he calm? Why? Why not?

_____

_____

3. Javier's parents and sister looked *worried*. Why?

_____

_____

4. When Spider arrived at Javier's house, he looked *pale* and *frightened*. Why?

_____

_____

5. Abuela sounded very *brave*. Was she?

_____

_____

Practice using descriptive adjectives. Interview a classmate by asking the questions below. Write down your classmates' answers.

1. How do you look after taking an easy exam, *happy* or *sad*?

_____

_____

2. How do you feel before taking a difficult exam, *nervous* or *relaxed*?

_____

_____

3. How do you sound on the phone after sleeping eight hours, *rested* or *sleepy?*

_____

_____

4. How do you feel when you watch a horror film, *scared* or *calm?*

_____

_____

5. How do you feel on Friday afternoon after school is over, *glad* or *depressed?*

_____

_____

6. How would you feel if you found a $100.00 bill on the street, *surprised* or *worried?*

_____

_____

Building Your Vocabulary

Phrasal Verbs

Complete these sentences with one of the phrasal verbs below. You may use some of the verbs more than once.

packed up	dropped off	came out
picked up	hung up	drive up

1. Lupe and Javier _____ their boxes at the end of the swap meet.

2. Abuelita and Javier _____ Lupe at her house after the swap meet.

3. Javier's mother _____ of the house when she saw Abuelita and Javier _____ after the swap meet.

4. Javier _____ the phone and then dialed Spider's telephone number. After talking to Spider for a few minutes, he _____ the phone.

5. Spider _____ Javier and Abuelita in his Chevy.

13 A Gang Confrontation

Read the chapter title and look at the illustration.

- ◆ **Where are Abuelita, Javier, and Spider now?**
- ◆ **Who are the other two men?**
- ◆ **What's happening?**
- ◆ **What do you think is going to happen in this Chapter?**

Careful reading: Now read Chapter Thirteen carefully.

A Gang Confrontation

1   "Where's your brother now?" Abuelita asked
Spider as they sped to their destination.

"One of his friends took him to the hospital. My
mother is there, too. She's been crying a lot. And she's
worried."

"Of course, she's worried," said Abuelita. "And you
need to help her stop worrying. You can help her and
your brother."

2   "I don't know if I can help," Spider said, "but I'm
going to let these guys know what's up. They shot my
brother."

"Do you know why they shot your brother?" asked
Abuelita.

3   "Oh, you know. It's one gang against another. That's
why. That's it. That's the whole reason!"

"But killing doesn't help anything. Killing makes
everything worse. We are fighting against each other
and not going anywhere. We are killing our own
brothers and sisters, for what? For what?"

"Listen, Abuelita, I know you're a good lady, and all
of that, but my brother was shot and I've got to do
something. You understand?" asked Spider.

4   "Yes, I understand. And I agree. You have got to do
something. That's why I came along."

"Abuelita, you don't understand," interrupted Javier.
"This is dangerous. Somebody might get shot. You
shouldn't have come with us."

5   "Believe me, even if somebody gets shot, even if I get
shot, we have to stop killing each other for no reason.
And to do this, we have to work together, not one gang
against another, but together."

But Spider had stopped listening. They were getting
close to their destination.

6   "Turn left up there, Javier, and go straight for about a half a block. Drive slowly. It's the place on the right, the one with the black pickup truck in front of it." Spider continued, "Pull over and park, Javier." Spider was beginning to sound nervous. Javier was nervous, too. But Abuelita remained calm in the back seat.

7   There was nobody outside. Spider started to get out of the car. Javier watched him and saw him check a pistol that was hidden under his belt. Javier took a deep breath, trying to be calm.

       "Where are you going?" asked Abuelita.

       "I'm just going to check things out," answered Spider.

8   "Just wait here. They'll come out, whoever they are. They know you want revenge for your brother. But they also know they didn't kill him. So they aren't too worried. They'll be out soon," said Abuelita.

       "How do you know about this stuff, Abuelita?" asked Javier.

9   "I've been around for a long time. I've been watching people fight for years. There are people fighting in countries all over the world. Some people keep fighting; others look for peaceful solutions. I'm always looking for peaceful solutions," she answered.

       "Shh . . . quiet," whispered Spider, "here they come."

10   Two young men were walking out of the building. As they walked toward the car, Abuelita opened her door. One of the men, looking surprised, reached for his gun.

       "You two stay in the car unless I call you," said Abuelita, to Spider and Javier.

11   Abuelita walked up to the two young men. One of them had his gun pointed at her. She continued to walk toward them. Spider, in the car, had taken out his gun and was covering her from the car. Abuelita said in a loud voice, "You can all put your pistols away. I'm here to talk with you, only to talk."

12   The young man slowly relaxed his gun. From the car Spider and Javier could not hear what Abuelita was saying, but they saw that the men were carefully listening to her. Spider wanted to know what Abuelita was saying. He wanted to know what was going on. He jumped out of the car and began running toward the young men talking to Abuelita.

"I know you shot my brother," he shouted angrily. "You tried to kill him. Who do you think you are? I'm going to kill you. Do you hear me? And now I am going to kill you!"

13   "No, you're not, Spider. Not unless you kill me first," said Abuelita moving and standing in front of the two young men. I don't want to die, but I'm old enough, and I've lived long enough. None of you has lived at all. Don't you want to live to be fathers, to be grandfathers, to be old with your grandchildren? Now stop this. You must stop this gang madness. I know one of these young men shot your brother. But if you shoot him, then everything will only get worse. And what do you get? Nothing but more pain, more problems. Right here, right now, we're going to talk," continued Abuelita. "Put down the guns."

14   The young men all looked at each other.

"She's right," said one of the gang members. "We should listen to her."

And they did. They talked, and yelled, and screamed, and cried. For a long time. And when it was over, they finally shook hands. But it wasn't over; it was only a beginning.

15   Spider drove Javier and Abuelita home. On the way home, Abuelita didn't speak much. She was very tired. She only said, "We must continue, this is only a beginning."

Understanding the Text

What did you understand?

Think about Chapter Thirteen. Are the following statements
TRUE (T) or FALSE (F)? If the statement is false, correct it.

_____ 1. Spider, Javier, and Abuelita drove to another neighborhood.

_____

_____ 2. Spider's brother is resting at home.

_____

_____ 3. Spider's mother is with his brother.

_____

_____ 4. Spider is happy that Abuelita is with them.

_____

_____ 5. Spider is ready for violence.

_____

_____ 6. A black car was parked in front of a gang member's house.

_____

_____ 7. Spider had a pistol hidden under his belt.

_____

_____ 8. Abuelita was the first person to talk with the other gang.

_____

_____ 9. Abuelita got the young men to speak with one another.

_____

_____ 10. At the end of the chapter, the young men began to fight.

Look at Chapter Thirteen again. Answer the questions by skimming the chapter. Read quickly to find the answers.

1. **Skim sections 1-6.** Where are Javier, Spider, and Abuelita?

   a. driving in Spider's car

   b. talking at Javier's house

   c. parked in front of another gang member's house

   How do you know? _____

2. **Skim sections 7-10.** Where are Javier, Spider, and Abuelita?

   a. driving in Spider's car

   b. talking at Javier's house

   c. parked in front of another gang member's house

   How do you know? _____

3. **Skim section 11.** Where is Abuelita?

   a. waiting in Spider's car

   c. walking up to another gang member's house

   b. talking at Javier's house

   How do you know? _____

4. **Skim section 11 again.** Where are Javier and Spider?

   a. waiting in Spider's car

   c. walking up to another gang member's house

   b. talking at Javier's house

   How do you know? _____

5. **Skim sections 12-14.** Where are Abuelita and Spider?

   a. waiting in Spider's car

   c. shouting at other gang members

   b. driving to Javier's house

   How do you know? _____

6. Skim sections 12-14 again. Where is Javier?

    a. waiting in Spider's car   **c.** talking to other gang
                                                       members

    b. driving to Javier's house

How do you know? _____

7. Skim section 15. Where are Javier, Spider, and Abuelita?

    a. driving in Spider's car   **c.** parked in front of another gang
                                                     member's house

    b. talking at Javier's house

How do you know? _____

Interpreting the Text

*What **else** did you understand?*

1. Abuelita asked, "We are killing our own brothers and sisters, for what? For what?" What did Abuelita mean?

_____

_____

2. After talking, yelling, screaming, and crying, Spider and the other gang members shook hands. Why?

_____

_____

3. Abuelita said, "This is only a beginning." What did she mean?

_____

_____

4. Abuelita asked, "Don't you want to live to be fathers, to be grandfathers, to be old with your grandchildren?" Why did she ask the gang members this question?

_____

_____

5. Do you think Abuelita was brave? How?

_____

_____

6. Abuelita said, "I'm always looking for peaceful solutions." What are some peaceful solutions?

_____

_____

7. Abuelita got the young men to put their guns down and talk. "They talked, yelled, screamed, and cried." What do you think . . .

they talked about?	
they yelled and screamed about?	
they cried about?	

Building Your Vocabulary

Words in Context

Complete these sentences. You can find the correct words by reading the paragraph number in parentheses. Then fill in the crossword puzzle.

Across

2 Abuelita is always looking for _____. (paragraph 9)

3 The young men talked, yelled, screamed, and _____. (paragraph 14)

5 Javier turned left and then went _____ for about a half a block. (paragraph 6)

7 Abuelita said, "We must continue, this is only a _____." (paragraph 15)

9 After driving for a while, Spider, Javier, and Abuelita were getting close to their _____. (paragraph 5)

10 Spider's brother was in the _____. (paragraph 1)

Down

1 Spider wanted the other gang members to _____ what's up. (paragraph 2)

2 The young men were _____ when Abuelita opened the car door and stepped out. (paragraph 10)

3 Spider wanted to _____ things out. (paragraph 7)

4 Javier interrupted and said, "This is _____." (paragraph 4)

6 Abuelita said, "We are fighting _____ each other and not going anywhere." (paragraph 3)

8 Abuelita was calm but both Javier and Spider were _____. (paragraph 6)

New Beginnings

Read the chapter title and look at the illustration.

◆ **Where are Javier and Lupe now?**

◆ **What do you see?**

◆ **Why do Javier and Lupe continue to go to the swap meet?**

◆ **How do you imagine Javier and Lupe's future?**

Careful reading: Now read Chapter Fourteen carefully.

New Beginnings

1   Javier entered his senior year at high school. He didn't have to take English as a Second Language (ESL) classes in his senior year. English was still difficult but he had finished ESL. Now, he read long books in English and wrote compositions in many classes. There were still many words he didn't know, and writing sentences to express himself in English was a big problem. But with hard work, he could do it. He had learned a lot of English in school and at the swap meet. And luckily, Lupe often helped him with his English class.

2   Javier spent a lot of time with Lupe. They were always making plans for everything. They shared a booth at the swap meet twice a month. They worked hard preparing what they sold and many people came to their booth to buy the painted and carved boxes. While they sat in the booth, Javier and Lupe talked over all their plans. Javier planned to carve all kinds of different things out of wood—animals, birds, even lamps. Lupe could paint them and they would sell them at the swap meet.

3   They were saving money. Soon, Javier would have his own car. They wanted to get married, but they were waiting for the right time. Lupe wanted to go to the university. She was planning to be an accountant. Javier still didn't know what he wanted to be. He was planning to attend community college after high school graduation.

4   Spider wasn't planning for the future but he was staying in school; he wasn't dropping out. Sometimes Spider studied with Radislav. And Spider was going to graduate. He was very proud of that.

5   At school, students could see that life had changed for Javier and Spider. Javier's sister, Ana, had told them about the gang shooting and Abuelita's courage. People knew that Javier and Spider were more serious now, more grown-up. Abuelita held meetings with Spider's brother and other gang members. They were beginning to talk over their problems. They invited others to come to the meetings and discuss problems.

6   Abuelita also visited Javier's school to meet with the teachers and counselors. The teachers and counselors explained that many different cultural groups had problems. They said that everybody needed to work together toward a common peace. Abuelita saw that these were community problems. People needed to come together to solve these problems. It was a big, but exciting task.

7   Javier had found his place in Los Angeles. His place was with his wonderful family, his girlfriend, his school friends, and his school. He knew that there was a life for him here. He could speak English and work hard. He could work with others to solve problems and plan. Plan for the future.

The End

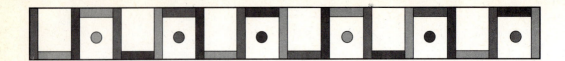

Understanding the Text

What did you understand?

Think about Chapter Fourteen. Are the following statements
TRUE (T) or FALSE (F)? If the statement is false, correct it.

_____ 1. Javier has to take another year of ESL classes.

_____

_____ 2. Javier is beginning to feel comfortable with all his
English skills.

_____

_____ 3. Javier and Lupe continue to go to the swap meet twice
a month.

_____

_____ 4. Javier wants to be an accountant.

_____

_____ 5. Javier and Lupe are planning to attend a community college.

_____

_____ 6. Spider is planning to graduate from high school.

_____

_____ 7. Abuelita is meeting with teachers and counselors to
work together on gang problems.

_____

_____ 8. Javier and Lupe are planning to get married in one year.

_____

_____ 9. Abuelita is meeting with gang members to discuss their problems.

_____

Discuss these questions with a classmate. Where did you find the answers in the chapter?

Example:

Javier has begun his senior year in high school. How is Lupe going to help him? (In which paragraph did you find the answer? __*1*__)

Lupe is going to help him with his English.
_____

1. Javier and Lupe have new plans for the swap meet. What are they? (In which paragraph did you find the answer? _____)

_____

2. Javier and Lupe want to continue their education after high school. What are their future plans? (In which paragraphs did you find the answer? _____)

_____

3. Abuelita wants to help solve gang and community problems. What are her plans? (In which paragraphs did you find the answer? _____)

_____

4. How is Javier feeling about life in Los Angeles now? (In which paragraph did you find the answer? _____)

_____

Real Life Skills

Continuing Your Education

When Javier graduates from high school, he plans to go to a *community college*; Lupe intends to attend a *university*. Maybe Spider will go to a *vocational school* to continue his education.

1. Where can you go in your school to get information about community colleges? universities? vocational schools?

   _____

   _____

2. What is the difference between a community college and university? What is the difference between a community college and vocational school?

   _____

   _____

3. How long do most students study at a community college? a university? a vocational school?

   _____

   _____

4. Where can high school graduates in your community go to continue their education?   Is it a university, community college, vocational school, or something different?

Name of school	Type of school

Building Your Vocabulary

Word Groups

Look at the school subjects listed below. Which subjects can you study at a community college? a university? a vocational school? Fill in the chart below.

education	auto mechanics	biology	chemistry
English	physics	plumbing	German
banking	sewing	dental hygiene	art design
business	fashion design	nursing	medicine
journalism	agriculture	accounting	cooking
electronics	painting	engineering	anthropology
sociology	construction	carpentry	ceramics
mathematics	sociology	geography	gardening
welding	law	food prep	aviation
architectural drafting	computer processing	computer programming	secretarial skills
catering	geology	nutrition	floral design

Community college	University	Vocational school

Thinking About the Past

What has happened to Javier?

1. Think about Javier's life since his arrival in the U.S. How has Javier changed over time?

   _____

   _____

   _____

2. How did Javier's relationship with Spider change over time? (Look back at Chapters 4, 8, 9, 10, 12, 13, and 14 for clues.)

   _____

   _____

   _____

3. How did Javier's attitude towards his life in the U.S. change over time? (Look back at Chapters 2, 3, 6, 7, 8, and 14 for clues.)

   _____

   _____

   _____

4. How did Javier's relationship with Lupe change over time? (Look back at Chapters 6, 7, 9, 11, and 14 for clues.)

   _____

   _____

   _____

Thinking About the Future

Let's Predict

Javier, Lupe, Spider, and Abuelita are planning their futures. What are their future plans?

Javier	
Lupe	
Spider	
Abuelita	

Javier, Lupe, Spider, and Abuelita have future plans, but the book ends here. Imagine that a year has passed. What has happened? Write another chapter by yourself, with a classmate, or as a class. Focus on one or more of these characters:

Javier	Lupe
Ana	Javier's parents
Spider's brother	Radislav, Spider's classmate
Abuelita	Spider

Word Recognition Exercises

Let's Practice

Look at the **Key Word** on the left. Read the other five words on the same line as quickly as you can. When you see the *same* word, cross it out and continue to the next line. Work as quickly as you can. It is faster to put a line through the word than to put a circle around the word. Time yourself or your teacher will time you.

Let's practice

Key Word

1. **read**	lead	red	reed	re~~a~~d	need
2. **five**	hive	fire	five	fine	hire
3. **one**	own	on	none	owe	one
4. **quick**	quiet	quickly	quick	quite	quietly

Practice again. After you finish,
- ◆ record your time at the end of the exercise;
- ◆ correct your work by putting a circle around corrections;
- ◆ write the number of correct answers at the end of the exercise.

Key Word

1. **play**	pay	pray	play	quay	clay
2. **sing**	song	sang	sung	sting	sing
3. **fun**	fin	fun	bun	fan	pun
4. **walk**	walks	walked	woke	walk	weak
5. **book**	took	cook	book	took	hook
6. **teach**	teach	beach	track	peach	team

7. **house**	mouse	home	house	honey	haste
8. **pencil**	peasant	pepper	pendant	pencil	penny
9. **desk**	dime	deck	duck	dust	desk
10. **chalk**	child	chalk	talk	cheek	choke

Record your time here. ⟶ Time: _____ seconds
Record the number correct here. ⟶ Number correct: _____ /10

Practice charting your word recognition progress.

10
9
8
7
6
5
4
3
2
1
0

How many answers were correct on the practice recognition exercise? If all 10 were correct, fill in the chart from the very bottom to the very top. If eight were correct, fill in the chart up to the line next to number 8.

60
50
40
30
20
10

How much time did you need to finish? If you needed 60 seconds, fill in the chart from the very bottom to the very top. If you needed 40 seconds, fill in the chart from the bottom until the line next to number 40.

When you do Word Recognition Exercises for each chapter of this book, try to increase your speed (go faster!) and increase your accuracy (get more correct answers!).

Remember . . .

◆ If you don't make any mistakes, try to go faster.
◆ It is okay to make a mistake when you are trying to improve your speed.
◆ Have fun improving your recognition skills. Good luck!

Key Word

1. **life**	bike	like	life	leaf	wife
2. **help**	helps	hike	heap	help	held
3. **woke**	wake	woke	make	weak	walk
4. **early**	earn	early	yearly	easy	easily
5. **chicken**	kitchen	kitchens	chickens	chicken	chicks
6. **yard**	yarn	guard	paid	darn	yard
7. **milk**	make	mike	mile	milk	made
8. **brother**	mother	brother	bother	better	brought
9. **school**	steal	scale	spool	school	scholar
10. **friends**	friends	friend	fiend	find	fiends
11. **door**	dare	door	dear	boar	bare
12. **parents**	patient	parent	patent	parents	patents
13. **toys**	boys	toy	toys	tops	tots
14. **country**	count	county	counties	country	countries
15. **letter**	better	ladder	liter	letter	gutter
16. **prepare**	prepaid	prepares	prepare	preface	precede
17. **trip**	strip	rip	tip	trip	trick
18. **new**	sew	few	won	when	new
19. **spoke**	speak	spike	spoke	spook	keeps
20. **thought**	though	thought	through	tough	thorough

Time: _____ seconds

Number Correct: _____ /20

Record the results in column 1A on the Word Recognition Progress Chart on page 188.

Recognition Exercise

Key Word

1. **them**	then	than	them	ten	hem
2. **home**	bone	foam	hum	dome	home
3. **mother**	mother	brother	father	bother	another
4. **story**	stony	stay	shady	story	starry
5. **born**	barn	bore	ban	born	bean
6. **house**	mouse	hose	house	noose	nose
7. **wind**	down	wand	wind	mind	nod
8. **whole**	when	what	who	whole	would
9. **better**	butter	latter	letter	batter	better
10. **young**	ground	yonder	young	youth	yolk
11. **walk**	woke	wake	weak	walk	week
12. **gift**	get	gate	golf	rift	gift
13. **gave**	gave	quiet	give	pave	jean
14. **night**	tight	might	height	night	right
15. **waved**	wave	moved	waved	made	raved
16. **knife**	kite	kind	knoll	knife	king
17. **pearl**	pear	pearls	pearl	pears	pedal
18. **their**	there	they're	then	their	them
19. **time**	team	tame	time	tin	tone
20. **school**	scale	school	stool	shale	cools

Time: _____ seconds

Number Correct: _____ /20

Record the results in column 1B on page 188.

1C

Key Word

1. **sunny**	bunny	sandy	candy	sunny	runny
2. **clothes**	close	cloth	catch	closet	clothes
3. **packages**	package	baggage	luggage	packages	picket
4. **received**	receive	relieve	routine	recall	received
5. **visited**	visitor	visor	visual	visited	visit
6. **wonder**	yonder	another	meander	wonder	wander
7. **dreamed**	dreamed	drone	dreams	drained	dreaded
8. **return**	retell	retain	recall	return	refrain
9. **happy**	honey	happy	hobby	hoping	hairy
10. **waiting**	weight	waits	waited	wanting	waiting
11. **outside**	inside	outsider	insider	outside	insight
12. **bread**	dread	breed	dead	bead	bread
13. **comfort**	comfort	confront	concert	conform	confirm
14. **going**	gong	gang	growing	going	pang
15. **depend**	pendant	deepen	drape	depend	depends
16. **journey**	joyful	journey	jogger	jewelry	journal
17. **nice**	niece	mice	ice	nice	cane
18. **small**	smell	small	smack	smoke	smile
19. **son**	can	sun	sane	son	seen
20. **started**	darted	stood	trash	street	started

Time: _____ seconds
Number Correct: _____ /20

Record the results in column 1C on page 188.

Recognition Exercise

2A

Key Word

1. **awoke**	awake	awaken	awoke	woke	wake
2. **lay**	lie	law	lay	bay	pay
3. **bed**	bid	bad	bib	bed	fed
4. **smell**	smell	smile	smoke	smells	smiles
5. **let**	bet	let	lit	lot	late
6. **got**	get	gut	got	goat	gate
7. **home**	home	bone	ham	bane	down
8. **shady**	share	shy	shade	shady	show
9. **fruit**	frail	trail	trait	fruit	fret
10. **busy**	dizzy	bus	busy	hazy	lazy
11. **miles**	mile	miles	nails	mail	male
12. **key**	day	hay	lay	key	hey
13. **cars**	core	care	cares	airs	cars
14. **learn**	burn	lean	learn	darn	loan
15. **new**	now	when	won	new	sew
16. **success**	succeed	succeeds	success	succinct	such
17. **had**	has	hat	bad	bat	had
18. **hurry**	hairy	hurry	furry	curry	worry
19. **people**	purple	palace	peace	place	people
20. **inside**	side	outside	insight	inside	incite

Time: _____ seconds

Number Correct: _____ /20

Record the results in column 2A on page 188.

Key Word

1. **strange**	strong	strand	string	strange	stooge
2. **dreamed**	dreams	dream	cream	beaded	dreamed
3. **about**	around	bout	abound	about	abroad
4. **breath**	bread	breathe	breath	threat	brother
5. **certain**	curtain	ascertain	shorten	certain	cuticle
6. **sleeping**	leaping	stripping	flying	sleeping	string
7. **window**	window	widow	widower	windows	willows
8. **morning**	mourning	morning	meaning	warning	boring
9. **quiet**	quite	gate	quietly	quiet	quit
10. **places**	pieces	palace	please	peace	places
11. **crowded**	corded	crowned	crowded	crowd	crowds
12. **noisy**	noisy	nasty	noise	neatly	nosey
13. **full**	fill	fall	hill	hull	full
14. **speaks**	spokes	peaks	spoke	speaks	speak
15. **funny**	honey	bunny	phoney	funny	pony
16. **back**	book	duck	deck	beak	back
17. **just**	gust	post	past	just	ghost
18. **here**	hair	here	hear	dear	bear
19. **happens**	hopping	happily	happen	happens	hoping
20. **wait**	mate	note	wrote	wait	meet

Time: _____ seconds

Number Correct: _____ /20

Record the results in column 2B on page 188.

Recognition Exercise

Key Word

1. **must**	mist	most	musk	must	moist
2. **went**	meant	want	wind	mint	went
3. **long**	long	lung	hung	king	lamp
4. **maybe**	mostly	maybe	marked	maple	major
5. **deep**	dope	beep	keep	deep	heap
6. **around**	rounds	round	about	around	arouse
7. **knew**	knife	know	knew	knives	king
8. **cars**	cows	stars	cans	cars	cabs
9. **feeling**	fooling	reeling	feeling	pealing	fainting
10. **think**	blink	thank	tank	think	thing
11. **like**	bake	look	like	bike	life
12. **see**	see	saw	sea	sin	seen
13. **what**	wheat	wait	where	what	where
14. **lonely**	lovely	lonely	loosely	loudly	lowly
15. **street**	stroke	stream	street	strike	steel
16. **where**	where	were	wore	wave	wear
17. **smell**	swell	snail	sneak	smell	small
18. **trees**	three	ties	trees	truce	freeze
19. **stomach**	stone	stake	touch	stomach	streak
20. **seems**	seams	seem	seems	smell	steam

Time: _____ seconds

Number Correct: _____ /20

Record the results in column 2C on page 188.

Key Word

1. **passed**	past	posed	passed	paced	pest
2. **want**	want	went	meant	mint	wind
3. **sorry**	story	stormy	sorry	sorrow	scary
4. **awaken**	awoke	awake	award	awaken	aware
5. **heard**	beard	hard	hear	heart	heard
6. **softly**	shyly	soft	softly	surely	sorely
7. **disturb**	destroy	disturb	distinct	dislike	dismiss
8. **room**	roam	rain	room	rail	ream
9. **saying**	sewing	staying	seeing	saying	sling
10. **slept**	swept	crept	creep	cleep	slept
11. **kindly**	blindly	kindly	highly	keenly	kidney
12. **obey**	ocean	ably	oboe	oats	obey
13. **yet**	bet	get	pet	yet	jet
14. **edge**	ego	edgy	edict	age	edge
15. **laugh**	tough	rough	bough	gauge	laugh
16. **maybe**	might	marine	march	maybe	mayor
17. **sound**	sand	found	sound	shamed	mound
18. **honest**	honey	honesty	honor	honest	hollow
19. **spoke**	spike	stake	spoke	speak	smile
20. **again**	about	around	admit	again	alien

Time: _____ seconds
Number Correct: _____ /20

Record the results in column 3A on page 188.

Recognition Exercise

Key Word

1. **new**	now	new	knew	mow	won
2. **called**	calls	call	called	cold	scald
3. **young**	youth	young	yonder	yearn	yogurt
4. **still**	style	stool	steal	stole	still
5. **speak**	spoke	speaks	seal	seek	speak
6. **glad**	gold	glad	glue	gland	glare
7. **disturb**	distress	disturb	dislike	distant	distill
8. **heard**	beard	hear	heard	herd	hurried
9. **mind**	wind	blind	rind	kind	mind
10. **what**	whale	where	wheat	what	wait
11. **obeyed**	object	obey	oboe	obeyed	obeys
12. **bad**	pad	bade	bead	bag	bad
13. **strange**	straight	strangle	strange	stripe	stagger
14. **laugh**	laud	laugh	launch	launder	laughs
15. **learn**	lease	least	leave	learn	leaves
16. **sound**	sour	south	source	sound	soup
17. **hands**	bands	hand	hands	lands	sands
18. **world**	word	worm	worlds	world	worse
19. **love**	leave	lost	live	lone	love
20. **grow**	grown	grow	growth	gown	grew

Time: _____ seconds

Number Correct: _____ /20

Record the results in column 3B on page 188.

3C

Key Word

1. **skin**	slim	shame	scream	skin	skate
2. **believe**	relive	relieve	belief	belated	believe
3. **many**	money	nanny	mean	may	many
4. **hope**	happy	nope	nape	hope	hail
5. **same**	sane	mace	seam	same	came
6. **given**	gate	gone	gave	game	given
7. **carried**	carted	carded	carried	curved	curry
8. **boxes**	backs	boxes	buses	bases	docks
9. **wooden**	would	nodded	wooded	wooden	muddy
10. **today**	toad	today	tooled	taken	tailor
11. **carve**	curve	carve	scarf	crave	course
12. **first**	fast	face	fist	first	flags
13. **ago**	age	ego	ago	aged	again
14. **pocket**	packet	pocket	picket	peaked	peeled
15. **tonight**	tight	tongue	tonic	tonight	tonights
16. **ready**	really	ready	needy	readily	reality
17. **where**	wear	when	wheel	whale	where
18. **father**	feather	father	heather	fatter	feature
19. **begin**	began	begun	being	begin	beggar
20. **wood**	wand	wind	wood	hood	wool

Time: _____ seconds

Number Correct: _____ /20

Record the results in column 3C on page 188.

Recognition Exercise

Key word

1. **kitchen**	kitchens	chickens	kitchen	kittens	sketch
2. **bread**	breed	dread	break	bread	drab
3. **office**	official	opposite	officer	offices	office
4. **register**	registrar	register	regal	registers	royalty
5. **clerk**	cloud	crowd	cloak	creek	clerk
6. **translate**	transfer	trains	trails	translate	traps
7. **forms**	from	frame	freight	fame	forms
8. **best**	rest	bait	beat	beast	best
9. **finish**	final	finish	finite	funny	finished
10. **smiled**	smoked	scaled	smelled	smiled	smiles
11. **attend**	attire	attuned	arrive	altered	attend
12. **public**	bubble	puddle	public	bundle	private
13. **shots**	shot	shout	shouts	shots	shores
14. **black**	block	brake	blade	back	black
15. **pants**	pant	pants	banks	peeks	peaks
16. **shake**	shook	stood	steak	shakes	shake
17. **help**	hope	heap	kelp	help	keep
18. **grin**	grain	pain	grin	green	prince
19. **been**	deem	dim	bean	been	bone
20. **staff**	stove	stale	fast	false	staff

Time: _____ seconds

Number Correct: _____ /20

Record the results in column 4A on page 188.

4B

Key word

1. **heart**	heat	cart	harp	heals	heart
2. **guys**	pays	buys	days	guys	rays
3. **whole**	hail	where	holes	when	whole
4. **people**	purple	steeple	pails	people	peace
5. **over**	rove	oil	oar	very	over
6. **turn**	tame	ruin	turn	tone	torn
7. **around**	about	round	route	around	aloud
8. **down**	done	down	bound	brown	dawn
9. **yard**	yards	jails	jade	yard	quad
10. **bench**	beach	breach	bread	dutch	bench
11. **there**	then	their	there	share	chair
12. **stand**	stale	state	stood	stand	steer
13. **thanks**	shanks	thank	tanks	thanks	banks
14. **guess**	queens	quick	gases	press	guess
15. **mine**	mane	name	moan	mine	nine
16. **almost**	already	almost	although	alms	toast
17. **family**	famine	family	funny	honey	famous
18. **proof**	roofs	proves	proved	proofs	proof
19. **mumps**	mumps	maps	mounts	numbs	pumps
20. **missing**	misses	missing	masses	meaning	naming

Time: _____ seconds

Number Correct: _____ /20

Record the results in column 4B on page 188.

Recognition Exercise

Key word

1.	**clinics**	cleans	creams	clinic	clinics	claims
2.	**visit**	server	visor	visits	visit	veils
3.	**free**	fee	freer	hear	foam	free
4.	**list**	least	risk	leak	list	teal
5.	**leave**	left	leave	leaves	leaf	loafs
6.	**problem**	problem	pavement	garment	problems	goblet
7.	**schedules**	scared	schedules	schools	scales	share
8.	**waited**	weighted	weight	mated	waited	weak
9.	**studied**	scaled	straight	studied	stream	starred
10.	**close**	cloth	shoes	choose	chose	close
11.	**home**	hail	mole	home	shone	name
12.	**fee**	free	fee	file	tea	for
13.	**charge**	shale	charges	charge	change	changes
14.	**ride**	raid	maid	made	read	ride
15.	**together**	tooth	gather	together	gander	towards
16.	**most**	must	most	toast	storm	musk
17.	**looking**	leaking	lake	leaning	looking	taking
18.	**back**	cake	bake	backs	beaked	back
19.	**soon**	same	came	some	song	soon
20.	**children**	children	chicken	heathen	chiles	child

Time: _____ seconds

Number Correct: _____ /20

Record the results in column 4C on page 188.

5A

Key word

1. **five**	fine	faint	give	five	fair
2. **block**	black	broke	block	bleak	bleach
3. **sister**	system	disaster	stern	sister	sisters
4. **story**	glory	starry	story	stormy	stately
5. **residential**	president	residents	residential	resolve	resolute
6. **street**	straight	stream	dream	greets	street
7. **building**	buildings	built	guilty	building	builds
8. **waiting**	meeting	wailing	waiting	weekly	healing
9. **young**	bound	ground	hound	young	gang
10. **babies**	bounds	drowned	babble	bubble	babies
11. **hour**	hang	your	hour	hand	scour
12. **name**	amen	mane	nail	name	need
13. **window**	winds	window	minnow	winter	mirror
14. **replied**	request	relax	reaped	replies	replied
15. **spoke**	steak	speak	spoke	provoke	speaks
16. **door**	bore	tore	roar	date	door
17. **station**	states	stationed	stately	station	straight
18. **wonder**	wonder	wander	meander	ponder	mentor
19. **through**	though	through	thorough	threw	tough
20. **scale**	stale	pale	steal	scale	scoop

Time: _____ seconds

Number Correct: _____ /20

Record the results in column 5A on page 188.

Recognition Exercise

Key word

1.	**weigh**	weighs	height	weigh	tough	bough
2.	**mouth**	moth	month	nothing	mouth	weight
3.	**trying**	buying	tying	paying	taking	trying
4.	**born**	down	dawn	barn	born	horn
5.	**city**	shady	cites	silly	city	sunny
6.	**puzzled**	paved	muzzled	puzzled	pretzel	nuzzled
7.	**pointed**	painted	pointed	tainted	punted	rained
8.	**opened**	penned	opal	painted	opened	opens
9.	**sign**	nights	gains	signs	sign	signal
10.	**language**	languid	language	languages	linger	longer
11.	**nurse**	noose	horse	moose	names	nurse
12.	**visit**	void	volley	visit	vapor	veal
13.	**normal**	moral	morale	normal	hormone	number
14.	**showed**	showered	shower	shows	showed	shared
15.	**sleeve**	sleep	sleeves	sleeve	speed	slave
16.	**needle**	matter	needle	needed	nestle	weeded
17.	**shot**	shout	sheet	shot	slot	skied
18.	**hurt**	hound	bound	burnt	hurt	huts
19.	**taken**	kept	token	taken	keen	took
20.	**given**	trained	gown	gives	grown	given

Time: _____ seconds

Number Correct: _____ /20

Record the results in column 5B on page 188.

5C

Key word

1. **cards**	carves	scarf	scares	cards	card
2. **yellow**	mellow	bellow	hollow	yellow	holler
3. **sound**	bound	found	ground	hound	sound
4. **thought**	through	though	thorough	thought	brought
5. **move**	mover	more	ream	rave	move
6. **either**	either	eight	neither	wither	heather
7. **dear**	read	deem	dean	dear	done
8. **motion**	making	motion	notion	waking	nation
9. **arm**	more	aim	ant	arm	ram
10. **surprise**	sunrise	surprise	sunshine	present	supper
11. **minutes**	minute	nothing	minutes	hindsight	weaver
12. **never**	river	never	fever	nearby	winter
13. **doctor**	bother	tinker	doctor	dates	doors
14. **where**	when	whereby	whether	where	with
15. **clinic**	cleans	clinics	clutter	clinic	sink
16. **block**	bleak	black	block	slack	hatch
17. **quietly**	quickly	quite	guilty	quietly	quilt
18. **crowded**	crowds	crowded	crowned	coward	cloudy
19. **ache**	arch	after	ache	age	afraid
20. **because**	beacon	became	blanch	besides	because

Time: _____ seconds

Number Correct: _____ /20

Record the results in column 5C on page 188.

Key word

1. **placed**	placid	planned	pleased	placed	glaced
2. **ninth**	might	night	ninth	ninety	height
3. **grade**	braid	glaze	grace	parade	grade
4. **eighth**	either	eight	eighth	height	neither
5. **report**	resort	report	retreat	relate	repeat
6. **loud**	lead	late	load	loud	lead
7. **fast**	feast	fast	haste	hate	fate
8. **word**	word	need	north	weed	cord
9. **next**	text	neat	nest	next	most
10. **also**	alas	solo	lasso	almost	also
11. **hard**	heard	card	herd	hard	head
12. **ears**	each	ease	reads	ear	ears
13. **attention**	attitude	attorney	attendant	attention	attempt
14. **thought**	though	through	thought	trough	tough
15. **morning**	mourning	morning	mailing	mountain	mainly
16. **fighting**	flight	frighten	fighting	flying	flouride
17. **noise**	moose	nuance	notable	noisy	noise
18. **wandered**	meandered	wondered	wandered	wanted	walnut
19. **colorful**	colored	cloister	collection	colorful	collect
20. **posters**	pastels	pasted	posture	poster	posters

Time: _____ seconds
Number Correct: _____ /20

Record the results in column 6A on page 188.

Key word

1. **countries**	counties	coughs	couches	countries	coupon
2. **wall**	mall	nail	law	wheel	wall
3. **students**	students	stately	student	studied	studies
4. **wonder**	wonder	wander	mountain	mounted	wooded
5. **liked**	hiked	liked	kicked	picked	leaked
6. **sounded**	shouted	counted	grounded	sounded	scouted
7. **sunny**	sandy	honey	sunny	cloudy	rainy
8. **different**	differed	different	definite	deflate	deflect
9. **face**	space	feast	face	haze	nice
10. **sudden**	studious	subject	submerse	suffering	sudden
11. **stopped**	stripped	stopped	streaked	toppled	stump
12. **vision**	mission	treason	visit	vision	visions
13. **real**	meal	heal	peel	read	real
14. **beautiful**	bountiful	beautiful	colorful	beauty	beautify
15. **angel**	angle	eagle	beagle	angel	anger
16. **stared**	starred	steered	stalled	stared	treats
17. **desk**	dusk	dust	deck	best	desk
18. **pencil**	pencils	gentle	pencil	painted	picnic
19. **questions**	mentions	tensions	citations	questions	pension
20. **oval**	oral	aural	oval	owl	value

Time: _____ seconds

Number Correct: _____ /20

Record the results in column 6B on page 188.

Recognition Exercise

Key word

1.	**thick**	think	thigh	chick	thick	three
2.	**hair**	hear	bear	bear	lair	hair
3.	**wore**	ear	wear	wean	wore	near
4.	**lipstick**	limber	limelight	lipstick	likeness	liquid
5.	**fact**	fast	feast	feat	fact	fate
6.	**slightly**	spring	lightly	slightly	straight	flight
7.	**turned**	burned	headed	tuned	turned	teased
8.	**felt**	fate	help	heat	left	felt
9.	**embarrass**	embrace	emphasis	embarrass	entice	emblem
10.	**moment**	momento	mention	envelope	minimum	moment
11.	**again**	gain	against	again	eager	agent
12.	**special**	space	speak	soprano	special	spacial
13.	**behind**	detract	behalf	behave	behold	behind
14.	**friend**	fried	fiend	friend	find	frontier
15.	**heard**	beard	geared	healed	heard	learned
16.	**bell**	dell	deal	bold	bear	bell
17.	**rang**	ramp	rant	sang	bang	rang
18.	**watch**	watch	match	catch	rather	weaken
19.	**books**	hooks	looks	walks	books	beaks
20.	**classroom**	classmate	closure	classroom	classical	classify

Time: _____ seconds
Number Correct: _____ /20

Record the results in column 6C on page 188.

Recognition Exercise   163

Key word

1. **sisters**	system	sister	seasons	sisters	sweater
2. **went**	want	neat	wheat	wait	went
3. **into**	onto	into	over	untie	orbit
4. **school**	school	should	showed	scowl	scroll
5. **buy**	sky	boy	shy	buy	day
6. **money**	monkey	many	nanny	woody	money
7. **sure**	shore	soon	sure	sore	scare
8. **enough**	elephant	ignite	rough	enough	equal
9. **pay**	day	bay	hay	quay	pay
10. **noticed**	motioned	notice	noticed	notched	matched
11. **giving**	bring	given	grouping	giving	grocery
12. **cashier**	cashew	tastier	caster	cashier	carrier
13. **ticket**	token	buckets	packets	jackets	ticket
14. **know**	knife	knives	knees	know	knew
15. **stood**	stead	stood	steak	state	street
16. **line**	lane	loan	home	tone	line
17. **friend**	fiend	found	friend	failed	fouled
18. **walking**	wailing	waking	mailing	walking	making
19. **toward**	towered	found	tailored	downward	toward
20. **though**	though	through	tough	thorough	thought

Time: _____ seconds

Number Correct: _____ /20

Record the results in column 7A on page 188.

Key word

1 **himself**	herself	handle	handled	himself	belief
2. **gently**	tightly	gently	general	gentle	grant
3. **nodded**	needed	heeded	nodded	noodle	handled
4. **head**	head	bead	read	hood	lead
5. **continued**	country	counted	continued	controlled	candied
6. **coming**	company	mining	counting	coming	curly
7. **here**	hair	hear	here	hail	heel
8. **replied**	relied	repelled	retried	replied	retailed
9. **extra**	enter	exits	eatery	extra	evenly
10. **until**	unless	unite	untold	untrue	until
11. **asked**	atlas	after	asked	alter	away
12. **today**	totally	rodeo	roadway	today	really
13. **show**	shore	wash	wish	share	show
14. **where**	what	were	where	which	witch
15. **office**	officer	suffice	riffle	office	outer
16. **thank**	stank	thought	tank	thank	shank
17. **little**	lighter	riddle	middle	bitter	little
18. **worlds**	worlds	would	molds	wealth	wheels
19. **difficult**	distant	distress	direct	difficult	differ
20. **trouble**	bubble	treble	truthful	turban	trouble

Time: _____ seconds
Number Correct: _____ /20

Record the results in column 7B on page 188.

7C

Key word

1. **months**	months	moths	mouths	north	routes
2. **years**	yearns	years	gears	hears	bears
3. **explained**	expired	explored	expressed	explained	explicit
4. **smiles**	snakes	miles	smiles	smokes	sneaks
5. **aloud**	around	about	along	aloud	allied
6. **helpful**	hopeful	fruitful	helpful	truthful	handful
7. **easier**	evenly	eastern	earthy	easier	eating
8. **arrivals**	arrows	arrange	arrival	arsenal	arrivals
9. **foreign**	favorite	failure	foreign	flavor	fortress
10. **helped**	heaped	hoped	molded	reaped	helped
11. **guess**	quest	queen	grown	guess	guest
12. **lucky**	mucky	lucky	lively	lonely	leaped
13. **both**	bath	hope	path	beach	both
14. **meeting**	wedding	weather	meeting	matching	melting
15. **club**	cloth	stop	hold	club	colt
16. **planning**	planning	pleasing	plenary	peeling	picnic
17. **costumes**	customs	suction	costumes	clothes	crafts
18. **carnival**	cannibal	countries	counties	carnival	candle
19. **festival**	refresh	fashion	fellows	fencing	festival
20. **check**	cheek	choke	chalk	check	cheat

Time: _____ seconds

Number Correct: _____ /20

Record the results in column 7C on page 188.

Key word

1. **chose**	cheese	choice	choose	chose	close
2. **packages**	package	garbage	mirages	packages	mileage
3. **tray**	gray	try	tray	fray	pray
4. **shy**	cry	lay	ray	shy	say
5. **carton**	cartoon	wanton	mortar	carton	traitor
6. **tasted**	toasted	treated	tailored	wasted	tasted
7. **food**	mood	fade	load	food	feet
8. **guys**	buys	rays	buys	days	guys
9. **grin**	gun	brim	train	gain	grin
10. **hand**	band	hand	wand	land	sand
11. **names**	manes	rains	names	wands	means
12. **some**	same	some	seam	soon	sand
13. **happy**	poppy	hippie	hoping	holly	happy
14. **whose**	shows	horse	where	whose	hours
15. **from**	from	frame	fame	fund	foam
16. **introduce**	interfere	introduce	interpret	intercede	indeed
17. **moved**	mound	month	moved	woven	weaved
18. **small**	smell	small	walls	smile	smear
19. **surprised**	supposed	surprised	surround	salivate	swept
20. **outside**	outer	inside	ourselves	outside	court

Time: _____ seconds
Number Correct: _____ /20

Record the results in column 8A on page 188.

Key word

1. **awhile**	whale	await	awhile	awful	award
2. **changed**	charged	changed	charade	chatter	charcoal
3. **saying**	crying	laying	paying	saying	herring
4. **relax**	relate	relax	relay	relent	release
5. **really**	really	readily	truly	burly	yearly
6. **fixed**	fined	lined	waxed	taxed	fixed
7. **short**	sheet	retort	short	shout	choke
8. **beauty**	bounty	lousy	beastly	beauty	party
9. **car**	tar	bar	car	par	war
10. **having**	heaving	having	craving	carving	hearty
11. **sixteen**	sweeten	between	sixteen	returns	kitchen
12. **waving**	waxing	weaving	meaning	waving	nearing
13. **later**	leader	later	ladder	latter	loader
14. **wondered**	wandered	wonders	wondered	weathered	neither
15. **wherever**	whenever	whether	weather	wherever	winter
16. **called**	sealed	soiled	coiled	cleaned	called
17. **drive**	drive	strove	drove	tried	boiled
18. **needed**	beaded	heeded	needled	needed	noodle
19. **just**	ghost	just	jean	gust	rust
20. **real**	reel	role	teal	veal	real

Time: _____ seconds
Number Correct: _____ /20

Record the results in column 8B on page 188.

Key word

1. **open**	onion	only	open	opaque	upon
2. **speaking**	spoken	peaking	spanking	speaking	spoiling
3. **happened**	hairpin	happiness	happened	hamper	handy
4. **morning**	mourning	noontime	microwave	morning	meager
5. **angry**	hungry	anger	anglo	angle	angry
6. **around**	abound	surround	toward	around	animal
7. **laugh**	load	cough	tough	pound	laugh
8. **minute**	motion	notion	minister	minute	million
9. **slow**	blow	plow	slow	lows	whole
10. **down**	down	dawn	doom	dame	dune
11. **nice**	rice	lice	mice	slice	nice
12. **wanted**	weaned	meeting	wailing	wanted	melted
13. **students**	stunted	storage	student	streets	students
14. **teacher**	reached	bleacher	teacher	treated	touched
15. **classes**	clever	clearing	clinical	classroom	classes
16. **helped**	heaped	hoped	helped	heart	heard
17. **anything**	amputate	ancient	analyze	anything	anyway
18. **late**	lost	least	hate	plate	late
19. **feel**	full	peel	leaf	feel	felt
20. **hurry**	hairy	furry	worry	sorry	hurry

Time: _____ seconds

Number Correct: _____ /20

Record the results in column 8C on page 188.

9A

Key word

1. **love**	lone	leave	love	dove	live
2. **drivers**	divers	driver	rivers	drivers	dribble
3. **license**	patience	likely	incense	licorice	license
4. **buying**	drying	crying	dying	boring	buying
5. **shown**	ashore	shown	shower	shame	showed
6. **impressed**	impress	empress	impressed	interest	incised
7. **nice**	rice	lice	dice	nice	mice
8. **promised**	palace	promised	praised	pleased	famine
9. **would**	wanted	wooded	should	would	could
10. **jumped**	jumped	bumped	dumped	numbed	lumped
11. **sound**	wound	bound	ground	round	sound
12. **daydream**	daydream	daily	bedroom	daytime	dreams
13. **voice**	vice	noise	raise	poise	voice
14. **repeated**	reaped	rotated	repealed	repeated	related
15. **interrupt**	interfere	intercept	interrupt	internal	except
16. **capital**	captain	corporate	captions	capital	candle
17. **quickly**	guilty	grandly	grapple	quickly	quake
18. **make**	bake	rake	sake	cake	make
19. **laughed**	louder	laundry	laughed	lounge	lately
20. **raise**	raisin	reason	raise	ration	rooster

Time: _____ seconds

Number Correct: _____ /20

Record the results in column 9A on page 188.

Key word

1. **hand**	band	hound	hind	land	hand
2. **shot**	sheet	shoot	shake	shot	plot
3. **air**	ear	air	hair	eel	oil
4. **called**	coiled	culled	called	rolled	collide
5. **confident**	complaint	confident	constrain	contain	confide
6. **correct**	dormant	mirror	piloted	correct	crescent
7. **important**	impolite	improper	important	immense	inside
8. **pictures**	pitcher	pictures	pierced	pictorial	pigeon
9. **stack**	steak	stroke	steal	stack	stake
10. **folder**	field	folded	folder	falter	holder
11. **photos**	photos	phrase	please	physical	physics
12. **interested**	interests	interplay	interpret	interested	internal
13. **moment**	moments	mailed	nobody	moment	minute
14. **enjoyed**	entertain	enjoyed	energetic	enforce	enamel
15. **downtown**	downtown	brown	bought	downhill	dough
16. **during**	drain	boring	during	daily	daring
17. **together**	tighten	towards	together	tolerant	tomato
18. **replied**	tailed	weighed	replayed	replied	repress
19. **right**	might	night	right	tight	light
20. **waited**	waited	wanted	wedged	weaken	wedded

Time: _____ seconds

Number Correct: _____ /20

Record the results in column 9B on page 188.

Key word

1. **usual**	unusual	utility	usually	usual	unreal
2. **greeting**	pleading	bleeding	greatly	gravity	greeting
3. **nickname**	neckline	nectarine	negative	nickname	needle
4. **ride**	rice	ride	read	rode	raid
5. **anyway**	anything	anyone	anyway	anywhere	annoy
6. **folks**	yolks	jokes	balks	talks	folks
7. **upset**	unsure	upset	unify	uplift	upper
8. **matter**	neater	mother	neither	matter	madder
9. **trouble**	treatment	trailer	traitor	trouble	treble
10. **worried**	worthy	wounded	worried	wrapper	worship
11. **tattoos**	tattoo	tattoos	tailor	tattered	tricks
12. **gangs**	groups	fangs	gangs	bangs	ranges
13. **fighting**	lightning	failing	falling	fighting	mailing
14. **girlfriend**	boyfriend	general	gimmick	girlfriend	gaily
15. **either**	either	neither	wither	earlier	eagerly
16. **tonight**	toenail	tightrope	tonight	together	teacher
17. **kissed**	kisses	leased	kissing	kissed	kitten
18. **cheek**	check	choke	cheek	creek	crawl
19. **leaned**	loaned	latter	learned	leaned	looked
20. **answer**	unsure	answer	animal	swear	anxious

Time: _____ seconds

Number Correct: _____ /20

Record the results in column 9C on page 188.

Key word

1. **wonderful**	waterfall	windmill	wonderful	mouthful	grateful
2. **fixed**	mixed	faded	waxed	fixed	kicked
3. **himself**	himself	herself	handsome	handle	handshake
4. **changed**	ranged	change	strange	changed	chain
5. **painted**	painter	painted	grated	greeted	pointer
6. **replaced**	replied	restated	reported	replaced	rewritten
7. **enough**	entail	errors	ignite	enough	rough
8. **running**	sunning	raining	taming	running	winning
9. **money**	honey	money	lonely	namely	rainy
10. **laid**	load	lead	laid	leak	lake
11. **owe**	oar	owe	won	ear	oat
12. **brother**	bother	better	mother	brother	bather
13. **ropes**	reaps	rails	ropes	tapes	goats
14. **funny**	bunny	penny	sunny	funny	many
15. **words**	wades	wakes	wards	weeds	words
16. **family**	folktale	dainty	famine	family	frankly
17. **stuff**	staff	trick	stick	bucket	stuff
18. **downer**	drown	founder	trapper	downer	painter
19. **problems**	pounds	bouncer	problems	package	bucket
20. **face**	pace	race	base	mace	face

Time: _____ seconds
Number Correct: _____ /20

Record the results in column 10A on page 188.

Key word

1. **opened**	widened	applaud	opened	alright	pens
2. **slammed**	slammed	clapped	mapped	strapped	slapped
3. **table**	marble	harder	token	table	tricks
4. **surprised**	supposed	striped	surprise	surprised	sunrise
5. **fingers**	figures	fabulous	frighten	lingers	fingers
6. **elegant**	elephant	elegant	electric	elation	eloped
7. **shaped**	shapes	draped	maples	shaped	shopped
8. **growing**	brewing	growth	hailing	failing	growing
9. **write**	wrote	write	bright	might	wheat
10. **angel**	angle	ankle	angel	anoint	anklet
11. **improve**	industry	improper	informal	improve	impact
12. **strange**	strangle	street	strange	steeple	straight
13. **correct**	collect	contact	socket	correct	count
14. **forget**	failure	forget	feather	feedback	feature
15. **inside**	outside	insight	inside	ensure	entail
16. **strong**	strange	swing	spring	sting	strong
17. **wrong**	wrung	found	sound	wound	wrong
18. **help**	hope	kelp	felt	heat	help
19. **find**	find	found	kind	rind	wind
20. **never**	neither	weather	matter	never	neater

Time: _____ seconds

Number Correct: _____ /20

Record the results in column 10B on page 188.

Key word

1. **laugh**	leaf	rough	lecture	laugh	leash
2. **glad**	group	grip	grind	gross	glad
3. **missed**	misled	missed	mused	made	mold
4. **wise**	woods	size	pies	wise	lice
5. **life**	leak	file	life	lives	feel
6. **awhile**	along	alive	agency	awhile	above
7. **longer**	holder	plunder	larger	latter	longer
8. **secrets**	special	screen	screw	scream	secrets
9. **already**	already	appetite	altar	altogether	always
10. **smiled**	aside	smoked	smiled	stroked	stroked
11. **back**	back	rack	lack	break	pack
12. **with**	myth	with	wrath	thin	milk
13. **spider**	shores	spokes	spider	spindle	slight
14. **talking**	walking	parking	making	talking	sulking
15. **used**	mused	sued	used	fused	usual
15. **there**	their	there	they're	thrive	think
16. **large**	charge	purge	merge	large	leader
17. **know**	know	kneel	knead	knife	knew
18. **school**	secret	stool	steal	scholar	school
19. **speaks**	spires	spokes	spoke	speaks	squeaks
20. **girls**	gates	girls	curls	purple	pails

Time: _____ seconds
Number Correct: _____ /20

Record the results in column 10C on page 188.

11A

Key word

1. **passed**	paused	poured	passed	gassed	based
2. **surprised**	surpassed	surveyed	surfaced	surprised	surely
3. **local**	vocal	local	musical	likely	lonely
4. **earning**	earring	earlier	earning	earnest	easily
5. **groceries**	groceries	pharmacy	pacific	gallantly	garbage
6. **tips**	tops	tips	hips	rips	nips
7. **chances**	changes	charges	chances	cheeses	chooses
8. **difficult**	directed	different	difficulty	difficult	dictate
9. **job**	box	tab	jab	jeep	job
10. **practice**	politics	graphics	quality	practice	polish
11. **awhile**	await	while	awful	away	awhile
12. **four**	fear	feel	foul	four	fuel
13. **plans**	peels	plots	plans	glades	blast
14. **customer**	contrary	costume	curfews	customer	cosmic
15. **working**	walking	making	waking	workday	working
16. **once**	ounce	opens	oust	outcome	once
17. **waited**	waited	water	mailed	waist	wasted
18. **drive**	drove	dive	drive	bribe	drives
19. **future**	feature	feather	nurture	future	father
20. **able**	edible	elder	able	abide	abroad

Time: _____ seconds

Number Correct: _____ /20

Record the results in column 11A on page 188.

Recognition Exercise

Key word

1.	**mind**	wind	rind	sand	hind	mind
2.	**slower**	blower	plunder	slower	flower	powder
3.	**wrong**	write	whale	wheat	wrong	wheel
4.	**besides**	behind	resides	beside	besides	better
5.	**saving**	raving	seeing	giving	waving	saving
6.	**special**	spacial	spoken	special	spirit	scenic
7.	**secret**	scissors	secured	section	secret	segment
8.	**keeping**	keepsake	keeper	kidney	ketchup	keeping
9.	**minutes**	mismatch	minister	mineral	minutes	minor
10.	**better**	batter	putter	better	bother	deter
11.	**little**	litter	latter	ladder	little	lather
12.	**salary**	salads	celery	safety	salient	salary
13.	**over**	other	ever	oven	over	even
14.	**smiled**	smelled	smiled	sweated	sweet	smoked
15.	**greeted**	graded	greased	greedy	greeted	greeting
16.	**arrived**	arranged	arrested	arrived	arrival	carrot
17.	**lovely**	lonely	lately	lowly	lovely	loudly
18.	**wooden**	wonder	woman	wooden	moonlit	woolen
19.	**rose**	rise	pose	toes	raise	rose
20.	**flowers**	flavors	flowers	floats	florist	floods

Time: _____ seconds

Number Correct: _____ /20

Record the results in column 11B on page 188.

11C

Key word

1. **carve**	caves	scarves	carves	carve	serve
2. **boxes**	foxes	boxes	backs	bows	browse
3. **room**	ream	roam	room	rain	ruin
4. **top**	pot	tip	pit	top	tap
5. **pretty**	petty	pretest	pretty	greatly	greasy
6. **myself**	mouse	mystic	mystery	myself	mystical
7. **how**	who	how	mow	hay	ham
8. **glad**	grade	glade	bald	paid	glad
9. **returned**	retailed	returned	retired	retained	retard
10. **show**	shade	swan	sword	show	shot
11. **rose**	rise	rice	rode	raise	rose
12. **already**	alright	altars	already	readily	adjust
13. **music**	moonlit	musical	music	muscle	minute
14. **knife**	knight	kitchen	kittens	knifes	knife
15. **pretty**	greatly	petty	pretty	greeted	party
16. **whichever**	whenever	wherever	hereafter	whichever	whoever
17. **craft**	draft	craft	weight	crawl	caught
18. **crowded**	crowned	colored	cotton	crowded	coward
19. **antiques**	antique	antiques	ageless	anywhere	anxious
20. **sudden**	sullen	cousin	sudden	sadden	redden

Time: _____ seconds

Number Correct: _____ /20

Record the results in column 11C on page 188.

Recognition Exercise

Key word

1. **swap**	sweep	smog	swap	soap	seep
2. **meet**	meat	meet	moat	neat	mate
3. **sold**	seal	sail	sold	mold	cold
4. **boxes**	boxes	bakes	waxes	taxes	taxis
5. **carved**	caved	paved	cavern	carved	carton
6. **painted**	paints	painted	pitted	grated	granted
7. **also**	always	only	also	solo	await
8. **morning**	mailing	morning	nailing	masonry	mostly
9. **afternoon**	alternate	awkward	afternoon	adjustment	algebra
10. **enjoyed**	annoyed	embroiled	entailed	enjoyed	angry
11. **turns**	turned	burns	mourns	turns	ruins
12. **selling**	sailing	calling	falling	cooling	selling
13. **walking**	wading	waking	talking	walking	making
14. **busy**	fuzzy	dusty	duty	bounty	busy
15. **sale**	seal	tale	gale	sale	pale
16. **bargain**	barters	basement	barter	bargain	beauty
17. **prices**	proudly	drives	prices	parades	garages
18. **earned**	early	easily	earnest	earned	eagerly
19. **display**	dismay	replay	delays	destroy	display
20. **tables**	marbles	cradles	tables	babbles	muddles

Time: _____ seconds
Number Correct: _____ /20

Record the results in column 12A on page 188.

12B

Key word

1. **dropped**	cropped	dropped	wrapped	tapped	slapped
2. **parked**	packed	peeked	parked	marked	darken
3. **unload**	unwrap	unload	unless	unlike	until
4. **phone**	ghost	phony	ghastly	phones	phone
5. **third**	tweed	tried	third	threat	treat
6. **fifteen**	fourteen	fifteen	fiftieth	fights	fifth
7. **sounds**	mounds	rounds	hounds	sounds	pounds
8. **really**	rally	really	reality	rotary	realist
9. **strange**	straight	stronger	strangle	strange	stranger
10. **stomach**	handmade	storage	stomach	sandwich	stolen
11. **thoughts**	through	thoughts	thorough	though	thought
12. **minutes**	minutes	mindful	magazine	madness	minute
13. **receiver**	received	reprisal	reproach	receiver	relied
14. **calm**	came	psalm	palm	calm	realm
15. **silence**	balance	patience	silently	silence	signify
16. **listen**	lighten	listen	christen	lastly	highly
17. **terrible**	terrible	tighten	terrify	trouble	tremble
18. **gangs**	bangs	fangs	gangs	pangs	hangs
19. **waxing**	waiting	wailing	boxing	waxing	taxing
20. **outside**	inside	outrage	outlive	outlook	outside

Time: _____ seconds

Number Correct: _____ /20

Record the results in column 12B on page 188.

Key word

1. **quiet**	quite	queen	quick	quiet	quail
2. **voice**	purse	noise	curse	voice	worse
3. **appear**	appeal	appear	apple	apply	approve
4. **happened**	hindsight	tapestry	highlight	happened	healer
5. **standing**	stealing	standing	stranded	sailing	special
6. **himself**	herself	ourselves	himself	itself	hinder
7. **business**	bathroom	balloons	battles	business	bless
8. **interrupt**	interplay	interpret	interrupt	interstate	interim
9. **better**	batter	blotter	bather	better	bloated
10. **started**	straight	standard	crowded	crated	started
11. **danger**	delay	diminish	diapers	depend	danger
12. **exactly**	quickly	piously	exactly	expertly	erect
13. **brave**	grave	crave	drive	drove	brave
14. **stick**	steak	steal	stick	strike	spoke
15. **screech**	speech	screens	streets	screech	spiked
16. **pale**	pole	peel	pale	peach	peak
17. **frighten**	fainted	freight	lighten	frailty	frighten
18. **seat**	soak	seat	meat	neat	seas
19. **front**	grunt	trunk	paint	faint	front
20. **window**	walled	window	mailed	widower	widow

Time: _____ seconds

Number Correct: _____ /20

Record the results in column 12C on page 188.

Key word

1. **confront**	comfort	contain	confront	console	confer
2. **sped**	speed	bled	sold	spied	sped
3. **hospital**	hatred	hurried	hospice	hospital	heads
4. **crying**	drying	buying	praying	frying	crying
5. **worried**	married	buried	worried	worldly	dried
6. **agreed**	agree	again	agents	agreed	agitate
7. **guys**	gays	buys	days	pays	guys
8. **shot**	sheet	shout	shot	shop	smog
9. **another**	annoyed	enough	amputate	another	animate
10. **reason**	treason	reason	rebound	reacts	reality
11. **whole**	whale	wheat	white	whirl	whole
12. **except**	accept	exempt	except	expect	exists
13. **fight**	might	night	light	flight	fight
14. **against**	agency	agent	again	against	agents
15. **kill**	bill	fill	hill	kill	pill
16. **along**	along	alone	atlas	alters	among
17. **might**	sight	right	night	might	light
18. **believe**	believe	receive	beliefs	receipt	behave
19. **together**	tighten	leather	weather	together	twilight
20. **stopped**	stripped	stopped	tripped	cropped	tipped

Time: _____ seconds

Number Correct: _____ /20

Record the results in column 13A on page 188.

Key word

1. **block**	black	bleak	broke	block	bleed
2. **slowly**	slowly	simply	silly	stately	slimy
3. **pickup**	picnic	picture	pickup	pitcher	pilots
4. **nervous**	nonsense	normal	merchant	nervous	natural
5. **remain**	retain	report	record	remedial	remain
6. **check**	shock	cheek	strike	check	choke
7. **whoever**	whenever	whoever	wherever	whatever	hover
8. **revenge**	revenue	retrieve	revenge	revolve	revival
9. **stuff**	proof	staff	draft	stuff	puff
10. **solutions**	solutions	solution	resolution	revolution	salute
11. **whisper**	prosper	wonders	thistle	whisper	whether
12. **building**	bouquet	broaden	building	delighted	built
13. **pointed**	painted	appoint	fainted	grounded	pointed
14. **surprise**	furnish	polish	surprise	tainted	surpass
15. **covering**	count	sound	pound	covering	mount
16. **pistols**	pistols	pistons	pitiful	platform	pirates
17. **jumped**	jailed	jumped	jeopardy	jersey	jogged
18. **relaxed**	relayed	rejected	relaxed	retained	rejoice
19. **careful**	careless	cartons	carbon	careful	cashier
20. **loud**	load	cloud	laid	look	loud

Time: _____ seconds

Number Correct: _____ /20

Record the results in column 13B on page 188.

Key word

1. **longer**	later	latter	longest	longer	loudly
2. **stand**	stood	creep	street	strand	stand
3. **running**	cunning	sunning	running	winning	tanning
4. **unless**	useless	nonsense	outlaw	unless	until
5. **moving**	roving	weaving	moving	mowing	cunning
6. **young**	hound	young	ground	pound	wrung
7. **front**	grunt	faint	frail	trunk	front
8. **lived**	dived	mined	moved	lined	lived
9. **fathers**	father	farther	fathers	fatter	lather
10. **madness**	nonsense	madness	madame	needless	seedless
11. **shoot**	sheet	shout	shake	shoot	shook
12. **worse**	worse	waste	roast	write	mouse
13. **pain**	gain	pain	vain	rain	pail
14. **yelled**	yelled	yellow	yearly	yonder	young
15. **scream**	dream	cream	learn	scream	search
16. **cried**	dried	cried	fried	wired	hired
17. **beginning**	belonging	beginner	beginning	bleaching	design
18. **continue**	complex	complain	compass	continue	carton
19. **over**	over	oven	after	oxen	only
20. **hands**	bands	hands	lands	sands	plans

Time: _____ seconds
Number Correct: _____ /20

Record the results in column 13C on page 188.

Key word

1. **entered**	entrance	emblem	entered	entrench	exact
2. **senior**	sailor	counter	senile	senior	censor
3. **year**	bear	dear	tear	pear	year
4. **books**	looks	hooks	socks	books	backs
5. **write**	wrote	waits	write	whale	wheat
6. **words**	wades	maids	nodes	words	waits
7. **sentences**	sentence	patience	nonsense	sentences	senses
8. **problem**	problem	complete	grounds	preamble	prefers
9. **making**	taking	dating	making	knitting	knotting
10. **shared**	shared	shores	shares	chairs	should
11. **booth**	bathe	tooth	booth	faith	teeth
12. **painted**	pointed	painted	peeled	grounded	dainty
13. **twice**	twins	tails	twice	trail	dice
14. **wood**	weed	tool	mood	food	wood
15. **saving**	raving	giving	sewing	saving	naming
16. **money**	maniac	namely	money	mainly	honey
17. **married**	worried	hurried	marries	married	carried
18. **talked**	walked	parked	talked	caulked	taken
19. **right**	might	tight	light	night	right
20. **classes**	courses	clashes	crashes	classes	classics

Time: _____ seconds
Number Correct: _____ /20

Record the results in column 14A on page 188.

14B

Key word

1. **university**	universal	unicycle	university	uniformly	unify
2. **solve**	crave	solve	carve	curve	save
3. **twice**	train	tweed	slice	twice	mice
4. **attend**	pretend	attain	account	attend	content
5. **college**	collage	college	collars	collide	collect
6. **staying**	praying	crying	frying	laying	staying
7. **dropping**	cropping	dropping	dripping	drying	hopping
8. **graduate**	garages	gradual	graduates	graduate	granted
9. **proud**	pride	ground	proud	grade	group
10. **students**	statement	student	stubborn	students	strings
11. **sister**	sitter	system	sister	slipper	sirens
12. **shooting**	shouting	throwing	hooting	shooting	shaking
13. **courage**	garage	courtyard	counted	counting	courage
14. **meetings**	footing	meeting	settings	meetings	mailing
15. **teacher**	tailors	tackles	tickles	teaches	teacher
16. **counselor**	cougars	costumes	counters	counselor	couples
17. **member**	number	finger	gather	numbness	member
18. **found**	ground	hound	found	sound	pound
19. **family**	frailty	homely	famine	family	honor
20. **life**	live	line	loan	lame	life

Time: _____ seconds

Number Correct: _____ /20

Record the results in column 14B on page 188.

14C

Key word

1. **English**	England	English	Empire	Evelyn	Ernest
2. **solve**	solve	caved	should	salute	salve
3. **others**	authors	antlers	emblems	others	elders
4. **future**	failure	future	further	futile	feature
5. **place**	plans	peace	piece	place	please
6. **speak**	spoke	steal	speak	spike	strike
7. **plan**	clan	gland	pail	plan	pale
8. **visit**	violet	virus	visit	vines	virtue
9. **work**	wake	woke	weak	work	wheel
10. **new**	now	when	win	not	new
11. **finish**	varnish	tarnish	parish	finish	marsh
12. **still**	stole	steal	steel	style	still
13. **problem**	painted	probable	possible	problem	preach
14. **things**	things	thongs	thinks	thoughts	stings
15. **would**	could	should	would	pound	molded
16. **know**	knife	known	knee	knight	know
17. **what**	wheat	while	what	whole	which
18. **compose**	comprise	compose	compile	complete	combo
19. **difficult**	different	diffident	difficult	diffusion	bullet
20. **end**	and	undo	end	ail	each

Time: _____ seconds

Number Correct: _____ /20

Record the results in column 14C on page 188.

Word Recognition Progress Chart

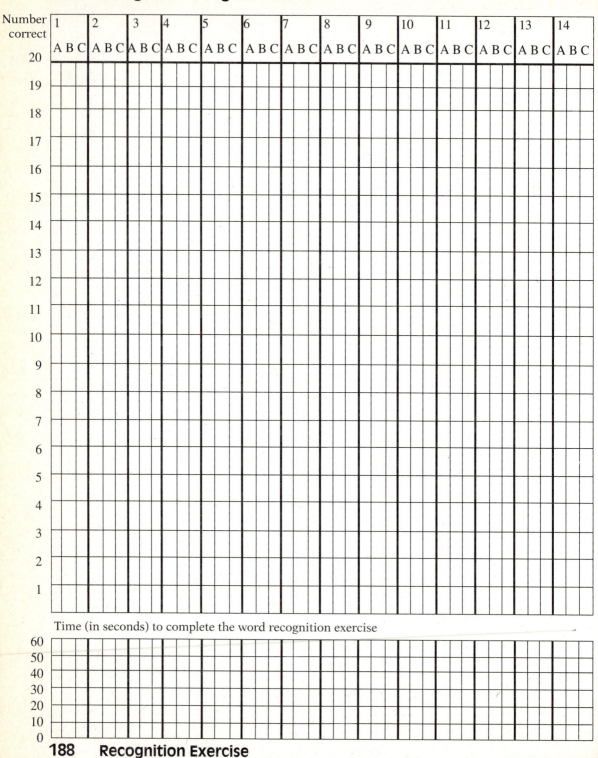

Number correct

Time (in seconds) to complete the word recognition exercise

188   Recognition Exercise

The Whole Story

1. Javier in Jalisco

This is the story of Javier. Javier was born in Guadalajara, a city in Jalisco, Mexico. Javier lived with his mother and father, his grandmother, and his younger sister, Ana. They all lived together in a small, adobe house. The house was surrounded by many large, green trees. The sun filled the house with light. The wind made the house nice and cool.

When Javier was five years old, his mother and father moved to Los Angeles, California. They left Javier and his sister with Abuelita, their grandmother. Javier's parents told him that they were going to California to find a better life for the whole family. Javier did not understand. He was too young. He was sad to say good-bye to his parents. Señor Flores took Javier for a walk before he went to California. He gave him a small knife with a pearl handle.

"Here is a gift, son," he said. "I'll see you soon. Your mother and I will send for you as soon as we can." Señor Flores gave Javier a hug. "Everyone is depending on you and your sister. Be a good son."

That night, Javier and Ana waved good-bye to their mother and father. Javier's mother and father started their journey to Los Angeles.

In Jalisco, Javier lived a good life with his grandmother. Javier loved his Abuelita. He always tried to help her in the house. Each morning he woke up early and went outside to feed the chickens in the yard. Then, he went back into the house and washed his hands and face. He ate his breakfast of bread and warm milk, said good-bye to Abuelita, and walked with his sister, Ana, to school.

At school, Javier and Ana had many friends. They all laughed and talked together. The *maestra* greeted them at the door. Life was happy for Javier and his sister. Javier always felt comfortable at home with his family and at school with his friends.

Nine years passed. Javier still missed his parents, but he was growing up. His parents visited him at Christmas time every year. He was accustomed to living with his grandmother. He often received letters from his mother and father. Sometimes his parents sent packages with clothes and toys. He was waiting to go to California to see his parents.

Javier dreamed about life in the United States. He wondered about the U.S.A., a foreign country, where people spoke English.

One sunny day, Javier returned from school. He found a letter from his father, Señor Flores. The letter said that it was time for Javier and Ana to come to Los Angeles. Javier was very happy. He began to prepare for his trip. He thought about his new life in the United States.

2. Arrival

Javier woke up. He did not remember where he was. Everything around him was strange. He lay in bed with a sleepy feeling. Slowly he remembered that he was in the United States. He had dreamed about the United States for a long time. He was really here. He took a deep breath and the smell made him certain; it smelled so different from the old house in Mexico. A small window let in the early morning sun.

Javier got out of bed quietly and went outside. Everything looked different, so different. At home there were big, shady trees, and fruit trees and places where he was able to see for miles and miles. Here, the houses were crowded close together, the streets were busy with noisy cars moving very quickly. Everyone was in a big hurry.

"So this is Los Angeles," Javier thought. "It is a place full of freeways, cars, and people. And I'll bet that everyone speaks English." Javier had a strange feeling in his stomach. He knew that he wanted to learn English. He knew that English could help him be successful in the U.S.A.

Javier went back inside the house. He sat down on the sofa. He was thinking. "I have just arrived. I feel lonely. I must wait and see what happens. Maybe I'll like it here but maybe I won't."

3. A Reunion With Papa

In the house, Javier passed the room where his mother and father were sleeping. He walked quietly because he didn't want to awaken his parents, but Señor Flores heard Javier's footsteps and softly called to Javier.

"Son, what is troubling you?" asked Javier's father.

"May I come in, father? I can't sleep," Javier answered.

"Tell me what is troubling you, son," said Señor Flores. Javier walked into the bedroom where his mother and father slept. He spoke softly because his mother was sleeping.

"Father, how can I go to school in this new place? I can't speak the language and I won't understand what people are saying to me."

"Javier," said his father kindly, "come and sit down here." Javier obeyed his father. He sat down on a chair near Señor Flores.

"Are you happy that we are all together again? Are you happy that you are in a new place?"

"I don't know yet, father," answered Javier honestly. "Everything is different from Jalisco. I have been thinking about the students at my new school. Do you think they'll laugh at me?"

"Maybe. Maybe some people will laugh at you. Your language is different, so some people might think you are different. You sound different. Maybe some people will laugh because they don't know what else to do. But you are not different; you simply speak a different language. You are the same person you were in Jalisco. Maybe we look a little different. We come from another place. People of all cultures move their hands in different ways or walk in different ways. Each culture has different customs. So in some ways, in our culture, we behave differently."

"You will see in school," continued Señor Flores. "The people in your classes will be from other countries. They will also feel strange. Perhaps you will meet other young people from Mexico, from El Salvador, or maybe from Southeast Asia, Russia, or Poland. I know it's difficult for you to understand, but believe your Papa; all people are the same under the skin. They are here from many countries trying to learn a new language and a new culture in a new place. That's a big job."

Javier nodded his head and smiled. The ideas his father spoke of were new ideas. Señor Flores had many things to teach his son. Javier began to feel happy thinking about his new life. He wanted to meet the new people at school from many different countries and cultures.

"But remember," Señor Flores continued, "all people are the same in one way. They want to love and they want other people to love them. They hope to grow to be good. They have to work hard to be good. There are many difficulties.

We fall down but we get up again. Always try to work hard to be good and to love others. Don't forget this and then you'll understand that people who look at you strangely are not so strange."

"Now, show me your pocket knife," said Señor Flores. Javier took the knife out of his pocket. He always carried the knife his father had given him long ago.

"Soon I will begin to teach you how to carve wooden boxes. You are old enough now that you won't cut your fingers off!" Señor Flores laughed. Javier laughed, too.

"I won't cut myself, Papa. I know how to use the knife."

"Good! Then maybe we can make boxes out of wood. But now, get ready for school. Today is your first day. Don't be late!"

Javier felt better. To see his father again, to hear him talk and to know that they were going to carve made Javier happy to be in the United States.

4. School Days

Javier got dressed and ready for school. He went into the kitchen and ate some bread and drank some milk. It was his first day of school. Javier's family went with him to school. Mr. and Mrs. Flores were taking their children to the office to register. The clerk in the office didn't speak Spanish, but she asked a student worker in the office to translate for the Flores family. The clerk gave them a lot of forms to fill out so that Javier and his sister, Ana, could attend school. The forms were in Spanish and English so Javier and Ana could read the forms and fill them out. They tried their best to finish everything. The student assistant smiled and said, "My name is Luz and I'll try to help you if I can." Javier and Ana were glad the student assistant was there.

"Have you had your immunizations?" asked Luz.

"Our what?" asked Ana.

"Your immunizations, you know, vaccinations. You have to be immunized to attend public school here," answered Luz.

"You have to get your shots!" said a voice. They all looked around to see a young man about Javier's age. He was dressed in black baggy pants and a white T-shirt. He wore a bandana around his head and on his left arm there was a colorful tattoo of a spider.

"Hey, I'm Spider. They call me Spider . . . just tryin' to help."

"Thanks," said Javier with a grin.

Spider reached out to shake hands with Javier. He said, "I know the ropes. I've been through this stuff. Maybe I can help you out. Where're you from?"

"Jalisco," said Javier. "Guadalajara."

"Oh yeah? I'm from San Salvador in El Salvador. The little country with a big heart," he grinned. "So you're from Mexico. There're a lot of guys at this school from Mexico. A lot from Salvador, too. I guess we've got a whole lot of people from all over."

Now it was Javier's turn to say, "Oh, yeah?"

"Well, see you around. Come on down to the yard and see me. I've got a bench down there. I can introduce you to some of the guys."

"A bench?" asked Javier.

"Yeah. I'm always standing at the same bench, so now I guess it's almost mine. Everybody calls it Spider's Bench."

"Well, thanks a lot, Spider. See you."

"Yeah, thanks, Spider," added Ana.

"Bring in proof of your vaccinations. You need a shot for mumps, measles and rubella," Luz explained. They turned back to listen to what Luz was saying. "And you also need a TB test and a DPT shot."

"Oh, I don't know if they've had all of those," said Mrs. Flores.

"If you're missing a vaccination, here's a list of clinics you can visit for your shots. Most of the clinics are free, but some charge a fee. You can call them before you visit."

Luz gave Mrs. Flores the list of clinics. Mrs. Flores put it in her purse and waited as Mr. Flores stood up to leave.

"Thank you, Luz. Thank you so much," the whole family said together.

"No problem," said Luz with a smile. "Come back as soon as you've had your shots and we'll finish your registration and give you class schedules," she said looking at Javier and Ana.

The Flores family said good-bye. They walked to the bus stop and waited for the bus. On the bus ride home, Mrs. Flores took out the list Luz had given her. They all studied the list, looking for a clinic that was close to their home and free of charge.

5. A Visit to the Doctor

The Glenwood Clinic was only five blocks from Javier's house. Javier walked there with his mother and sister. It was a small, one-story building on a quiet, residential street.

As they entered the building, Javier looked around. There were many people sitting in the Waiting Room. There were a few old people. There were also young children and babies. The Glenwood Clinic was crowded and noisy.

Javier gave the receptionist his and Ana's name. Then he sat down to wait with the other people. They waited for more than an hour. Finally, Javier heard the receptionist call his name.

"Javier Flores." Javier got up and went to the receptionist's window.

"Are you Javier Flores?" asked the receptionist in Spanish.

"Yes, I am," Javier replied. Javier was glad the receptionist spoke Spanish, but he wondered how he was going to learn English.

"Go through the door and you'll see the nurse's station on the left there," continued the receptionist.

Javier went through the door. He saw the nurse standing by a scale. The nurse put him on the scale to weigh him. And then, in English, she told him to open his mouth.

"You speak English. Are you from Los Angeles?" asked Javier trying out his English.

"No, I'm not. Actually I was born in Toronto. That's a city in Ontario, Canada."

Javier did not understand. He looked at her puzzled. Then the nurse told him to open his mouth. Javier still did not understand. So the nurse pointed to her mouth and opened it.

"Aha," thought Javier. She wants me to open my mouth. At least I understand sign language. As soon as Javier opened his mouth, the nurse put a thermometer in it. He sat down. She took the thermometer out of his mouth and read it.

"You weigh 123 pounds and your temperature is normal. Very good," the nurse said with a smile. "Now, let's give you your shots. Roll up your sleeve."

Once again, Javier did not understand. Once again, the nurse showed him what to do. Javier rolled up his sleeve. Then he looked at the tray with three needles on it.

"You'll be getting three shots," the nurse explained. "Your DPT, MMR, and a TB test."

Javier didn't say anything. The nurse took a big needle and gave Javier a shot. It hurt! It hurt a lot! But Javier didn't make a sound. "It will be over soon," he thought.

Ana was weighed, had her temperature taken, and was given her shots, too. Now, they were both finished. The nurse stamped a yellow card for each of them. The yellow cards were proof of their vaccinations.

"Okay," said the nurse, "you're finished. Come back when you've learned more English and I'll tell you about Toronto."

Javier did not move. Ana did not move, either.

"Oh dear. You didn't understand me, did you?" she said opening the door and motioning for them to leave.

Javier and Ana were surprised. They had waited for more than an hour and their shots had taken only five minutes. And they had never seen the doctor! They returned to the Waiting Room where Mrs. Flores was sitting patiently. They all left the Glenwood Clinic. Javier and Ana were glad their vaccinations were over. They walked home quietly because they each had an ache in their right arm.

6. A New Romance: Guadalupe

They placed Javier in the eleventh grade after registration. They placed Ana in the ninth grade. Javier took his class schedule and reported to his classes. As he sat in his class, his teacher spoke English. English sounded very strange and he thought the teacher spoke very fast. He didn't understand one word.

In the next class, the teacher also spoke English. He thought she spoke fast, too. Javier could not pay attention. His thoughts were leading him into daydreams. He was thinking of a sunny morning in Mexico, a morning when the chickens were fighting in the yard and making a lot of loud noise.

As Javier daydreamed, his eyes wandered around the class. He saw the colorful posters from many countries on the wall. There were posters from all over Mexico and Central America. There were posters from Southeast Asia, Africa, Russia, and many other places he had never seen or even dreamed about. He looked at all the different students.

"Where do they all come from?" he wondered. Some were from Asia. Maybe they were Korean or Japanese or Chinese. He didn't know. Other students were from different places and spoke different languages. He was looking at each face when suddenly, he stopped. He thought he was having a vision. No, it was real.

In the classroom sat the most beautiful angel he had ever seen. He wasn't daydreaming now. He was back in the classroom. He stared at the girl. She was sitting at a desk with a pencil in her right hand. She was writing. He could see her eyes as she looked up at the blackboard to read the questions. Her eyes were dark and oval. She had long, thick brown hair. She didn't wear any lipstick. In fact, she wore no make-up at all. Javier could not stop staring at her.

The girl seemed to feel his eyes on her. She turned her head slightly. He was embarrassed because she knew he was looking at her. They both looked down. But in a moment, they both looked up again. Their eyes met. The girl turned away. Javier looked down. He tried not to look at her again. She was so beautiful. He wanted to meet her. He knew she was special.

The bell rang and class was over. But a new romance had begun. Javier watched the beautiful girl pick up her books. She got up and walked out of the classroom with another girl. Javier tried to stay close behind them. He wanted to hear her voice. Javier followed them as they walked out of the classroom and down the hall. The two friends were talking. Javier could not hear what they were saying, but he heard her friend call her by name: "Guadalupe," she said. Guadalupe. The name of the beautiful angel was Guadalupe.

7. Lunchtime

It was time for lunch. Javier went out onto the school yard. He looked for his sister, Ana, but he didn't see her. So he went into the school cafeteria to buy his lunch. He didn't have a lot of money. He wasn't sure if he had enough money to pay for his lunch. He noticed other students giving the cashier tickets, not money. He didn't have a ticket and he didn't know how to get one. As he stood in line wondering, he looked up and saw Guadalupe and her friend. They were walking toward him.

"They're coming to talk to me," Javier thought to himself. "Beautiful Guadalupe and her friend are coming to talk to me!" He didn't say anything aloud.

"You're new here, aren't you?" asked Guadalupe, gently. Javier nodded his head.

"Do you have a lunch ticket?" continued Guadalupe.

"No, I don't," he replied.

"Well, I have an extra ticket and I can give it to you until you get your lunch tickets."

"You have an extra ticket?" asked Javier. "How did you get an extra ticket?"

"I brought my lunch from home, today," explained Guadalupe. She gave Javier the ticket. "You can use my ticket to get your lunch today. And after lunch we can show you where to get a ticket form. After you fill out the application and turn it in, the office will give you lunch tickets and you won't have to pay for your lunch."

"Thank you, thank you very much," said Javier in English.

"Do you speak a little English?" asked Guadalupe.

"Only a little," replied Javier. "Is the ticket form in English?"

"It's in English and Spanish. I can help you fill out the form. I can help you a lot with English if you'd like. When I came here from Nicaragua, I only spoke Spanish. And now I'm almost bilingual. That means I speak two languages and having two languages is like having two worlds. It was very difficult at first. I had a lot of trouble. I thought I could learn English in a few months, but it took more than two years," explained Guadalupe with a smile.

Javier returned her smile. "She is so beautiful. And she's smart, too," he thought with admiration. When he spoke aloud, he said to her in Spanish, "Someday, I hope I will be bilingual, too. You've been very helpful to me. I thank you for all your help."

"We try to help new students because we remember our own arrivals in the United States. It is difficult to come to a foreign country. You sometimes have a lot of problems with language, money . . . all kinds of things."

"Oh, excuse me, I forgot to introduce my friend. This is Tagui. She's from Yerevan, in Armenia. She tries to help new students, too. They need so much and there are so many different problems. Tagui and I try to help new arrivals like you whenever we can. It's easier to help you because I speak Spanish, but Tagui and I help each other practice English. We also help students from other countries, too. We've helped students from lots of places, like Vietnam and Iran, too. I guess everyone who comes here has a few problems."

"I feel lucky that I met you both," said Javier.

"Well, let us know if we can help you again. We'll see you later. We have to go to a meeting," said Guadalupe as she and Tagui began to walk away.

"You have to go to a meeting?" asked Javier. He thought that they must be very important people.

Guadalupe laughed. "Yes, it's an International Club meeting. Students from countries all over the world get together."

"What do they meet about?" asked Javier curiously.

"Oh, we plan all kinds of things . . . like food festivals and carnivals and fashion shows with costumes from different countries. And we talk about many different ideas from other countries. Today we're planning an International Folkdance Day. You're welcome to come to our meetings and check them out." She paused. "Well, we'd better go or we'll be late."

"Well thanks, thanks again," said Javier. "For the ticket and everything." He turned and got back into the cafeteria line. "I hope I haven't missed lunch," he thought. "I'm hungry."

8. On the Yard

In the cafeteria, Javier chose two food packages and put them on his tray. He didn't know what was inside the packages. He was too shy to ask anybody. He took a carton of milk and gave his ticket to the cashier. Javier sat down in the cafeteria and ate the food in the packages. The food tasted okay. He liked the spicy burrito and the green jello. After lunch, Javier went outside onto the yard.

On the yard, Javier looked for Ana again. He was surprised to see Spider. Spider approached Javier with a big grin.

"Hey man, how're you doing?" said Spider offering his hand to Javier.

"Let me introduce you to some of the guys." Javier looked around and listened as Spider told him the names of his many friends. Javier was happy to meet Chuy because he remembered that in Guadalajara he had a friend whose name was Chuy, too.

Spider introduced him to Radislav who was from Bulgaria. And then he met Byung who was Korean. Byung had moved from Korea to Argentina when he was small, so he spoke Spanish and Korean. Radislav spoke a little Spanish, too. Javier was very surprised. As they spoke to him, he noticed that they all spoke Spanish for awhile and then they changed back into English. Then they changed back to Spanish.

All of this was very interesting to Javier because he understood a lot of what they were saying. He watched quietly, but did not say very much. Everybody seemed friendly. Javier began to relax. Radislav was telling him about Spider's car. He told him that Spider had a really nice car. The car was an old car that Spider had fixed up, a Chevrolet. Radislav called it a "Chevy" for short. Radislav said that the Chevy was a real beauty. Javier thought about having a car. Soon he would be able to drive. He was almost old enough now. He just needed experience. With a car, he could go wherever he wanted. He looked at Spider. He thought about Spider's Chevrolet. He was sure that even an old car cost a lot of money. He wondered how Spider had earned money for a car.

As he was thinking, Javier looked across the yard. His sister, Ana, was waving at him. She had been looking for him.

"Hey, I've got to go, Spider," Javier said. "My little sister's all alone. I'll see you guys later."

"Right, buddy," said Spider. "See you, later."

Javier walked across the yard toward Ana. Before Javier could open his mouth, Ana began speaking to him.

"Oh, Javier, so many things happened to me this morning. I got lost on the way to my class. A student helped me find my classroom. But I arrived late and the teacher got angry at me. I started to cry and the helpful student put her arm around me so I wouldn't feel bad, but . . ."

"Wait a minute, Ana," interrupted Javier, "you're talking so fast that I can't understand anything you're saying. Slow down, slow down."

Ana began to laugh. "You're right, Javier. I feel like everything is happening so quickly. I only wanted to tell you that I have a nice new friend. Her name is Celia. She helped me a lot. She told me that the teacher is very nice but doesn't like students to arrive late."

"Don't worry, Ana," said Javier. "You won't be late anymore because you won't get lost anymore. You know your way around school now. I'm glad you made a new friend. I met some nice people today, too," Javier said. He was thinking of Spider's friends. He was also thinking of Guadalupe, but he didn't want to tell his sister.

The bell rang. "I have much more to tell you, Javier," said Ana. But I have to hurry to class."

"Don't be late! I'll see you after school." It was time to go to class.

9. Car Love

Javier spent a lot of time during the next few weeks thinking about cars. He thought about getting his driver's license, learning to drive, and buying a car. Spider had shown Javier his beautiful Chevy. Javier was impressed. The Chevy was a nice car. Someday, he promised himself, he would have a car like that.

"Did you hear me, Javier?" Javier jumped. He heard the sound of his teacher's voice interrupting his daydreams. "Javier?" she repeated. "Are you daydreaming? I asked you to tell us the capital of California."

"Sacramento," Javier said quickly. "And Detroit is the capital of Michigan . . . where they make Fords and Chevys."

Everyone laughed. The teacher, Ms. Silver, laughed, too. "No," she said "Detroit is not the capital of Michigan. And you're daydreaming when you should be paying attention. I'm glad you're interested in cars Javier, but we're working on state capitals now. Stay with us," she advised gently. "Who can raise his hand and tell me the capital of Michigan?"

Guadalupe's hand shot up into the air. When Ms. Silver called on Lupe, she said confidently, "Lansing is the capital of Michigan."

"That's correct, Lupe. Very good. But it's also true that Detroit is a big, important city in Michigan and they make a lot of cars there."

"I know, Ms. Silver. I have pictures of cars they used to make in Detroit. These are old cars," Javier said, taking out a large stack of photos from a folder. "Aren't they beautiful?"

Ms. Silver smiled again. She was glad Javier was so interested in cars. She thought it was important for students to have special hobbies. She took a moment from the lesson on state capitals to let Javier show a few of his photos. The class enjoyed looking at the old cars.

"Where did you get those pictures?" asked one student.

"There was an auto show downtown. I went with my Dad. They gave us all these photos for free. The show was great."

"Thank you, Javier," said Ms. Silver. "Now, who remembers where these cars were made?"

"Detroit, Michigan," a few students answered together.

"And what's the capital of Michigan?" she asked again.

"Lansing," the class replied.

"Right! And the capital of California, Javier?"

"Sacramento," said Javier. He was paying attention now.

"Right again!" said Ms. Silver.

The bell rang. Class was over. Guadalupe waited for Javier. Together they walked out to the yard.

"What's up?" said Spider walking toward them. "What's happening, brother?"

"Not too much, Spider," answered Javier.

"Do you need a ride home today? I'm driving right by your place."

"I sure do! Wow! A ride would be great! Could you take Lupe, too?"

"Sure, brother, no problem," said Spider.

"Oh, that's okay," said Lupe. "I don't need a ride. Anyway, my folks might get upset."

"Lighten up, Lupe," Javier said, putting his arm around her shoulder. Your folks won't get upset and I want you to see how Spider's Chevy drives. It's great!"

"All cars are the same to me, Javier," she answered. "I've told you already. It doesn't matter to me what they look like." She took his arm off of her shoulder.

"Uh, hey guys, I 've got to go. I'll meet you in the parking lot after school." Spider quickly walked away. He didn't like to be around couples when they were uptight.

"Thanks, amigo," said Javier. "See you after school."

"Yeah," answered Spider, "see you."

Javier turned to Guadalupe. She looked upset. "What's the matter, Lupe?" he asked her.

"I don't want to go in Spider's car. My father will get mad at me."

"Well, it's okay if you don't want to. I only wanted you to ride home with me. You know I like to be with you."

"I like to be with you, too, Javier. But not with Spider. He's trouble."

"What do you mean, Lupe? He's a good guy."

"I know he's nice to you, Javier, but I'm worried. He has those tattoos and I'm not sure if he's in a gang, but I know my father gets mad about stuff like that."

"Like what? Lots of people have tattoos. It doesn't mean they're in gangs."

"I know. But I'm pretty sure Spider is in a gang. He hangs out with all the gang guys and he, well, he acts like he's in a gang."

"Look, Lupe, why are we fighting? You're my girlfriend and I'm not in a gang. We don't have to worry about Spider," explained Javier.

"Well, we don't have to worry about him, if you don't hang out with him too much."

"Let's not talk about it anymore right now. Okay? I'll call you tonight."

"Are you going home in Spider's car?" asked Lupe.

Javier did not look at her. He did not say anything, either.

"Well, Javier, aren't you going to answer me?"

"I've got to go. I'll call you tonight." Javier leaned over and kissed Guadalupe on the cheek. She did not look up at him.

10. Abuelita's Visit

After school, Javier went home in Spider's Chevy. As they drove, they talked about the car. Spider had fixed the transmission himself and painted the car "candy apple red." Many of his friends had helped Spider work on the car. It was an old car and sometimes needed car parts replaced. But now, Spider was worried. The car was running fine and it looked fine, but he didn't have money to take care of it. He didn't have any money and he had lost his part-time job.

"I didn't know you had a part-time job, Spider," said Javier.

"Well, I don't anymore. They laid me off and now I don't have any money. I was thinking of selling my car. Or maybe I'll quit school and try to get a full-time job. I owe my brother some money and he needs it."

"I guess everyone has problems. I was thinking you didn't have any problems. You know, you've got this great car, you have so many friends, and well, you really know the ropes."

Spider laughed. "Javier, my friend, you are too funny for words! I have so many problems with school, with my family, no job, no money, and the gang problems. Hey, I don't want to talk about all this stuff. It's a downer!"

"Gee, I wish I could help you in some way, Spider," said Javier. "I sometimes think about dropping out of school. I need money, too. But Lupe said she'd break up with me if I dropped out. She says if you want to be somebody someday, you have to finish school. I don't know."

"Hey, everybody's got problems. We all have to face our problems. You've got yours, I've got mine. We do the best we can. Don't worry about it, my friend. You help me every time I see your smiling face. They drove along in silence for awhile. They were thinking about their problems.

Javier looked up. They had arrived at his house. "Well, here we are, at your house," said Spider.

Javier picked up his stuff and opened the car door. "Thanks for the ride, Spider. Your car is great!"

"Yeah, yeah," smiled Spider. "I know."

Javier shut the car door and went inside. When he went into the kitchen, he was surprised to see his grandmother sitting at the table. With her long, thin fingers and her strong face, Abuelita looked calm and beautiful. She was not a young woman, but Javier did not see her age.

"Abuelita," he said to her. "Abuelita, it's so good to see you." He went over and gave her a hug. Javier had missed his grandmother.

"How are you, Abuelita?" asked Javier. "I'm so happy you're here with us."

"I'm fine, Javier. I'm glad to see that you are growing. You look big and tall. Your father and mother tell me you eat a lot of food these days. That's good. And you go to school everyday. That's good, too. And what else?"

"Oh, many things, Abuelita. I have so many things to tell you."

"Are you learning English?" asked Abuelita.

"Yes, a little. I can say many things now. But there are also many other things I cannot say or write. English is very difficult."

"Of course it is. It takes people many years to learn English. And some people never learn; they give up. Do you have a good teacher?"

"Yes, I have many good teachers. And I have a girlfriend, a *novia*. She is very beautiful, like an angel. Her name is Lupe. She speaks English very well and she helps me with my English."

"I hope I will get to meet this Guadalupe angel. And I hope your English will improve. Now tell me about your other friends. Your sister, Ana, tells me you have two friends with very strange names. One is Spider and the other is, hmmm, let me see . . . Raslof, is that correct?"

"Spider and Radislav. Spider is from El Salvador and Radislav is from Bulgaria. Spider has a beautiful old Chevrolet. He wants to sell it and I'm going to try to buy it. I don't know how, but I'm going to try to figure it out."

"It sounds like many things have changed for you, Javier. You are growing up. Girlfriends and cars and money are nice things to have, but don't forget the important things you and I have always talked about. Don't forget to be good inside, Javier."

"Now you are talking like Lupe, Abuela. She doesn't like cars very much. And she doesn't like Spider, either. She says other things are more important, like being a good, decent person."

"She sounds like a very strong girl, Javier. I like strong females. Now I am sure I want to meet her. But, tell me, Javier, why doesn't Guadalupe like your friend, Spider? Does she like Radislav?"

"She likes Radislav because he doesn't have a tattoo or drive a Chevy. She thinks Spider is in a gang."

"And is he in a gang? A *pandilla*?" asked Abuelita.

Javier was surprised. He thought that his grandmother didn't know anything about gangs, but he was wrong.

"I don't know if he's in a gang, Abuelita. Do you know about gangs?"

"I know about gangs. Everyone has heard about gangs. It is important to know what is true about gangs and what isn't true. It's also important to find out if Spider is in a gang. Because if he is, he may be in trouble and need help. If you're his friend, you may have to help him."

"I'll find out. I'll find out if he's in a gang. I know he has a lot of problems, but he doesn't like to talk about them."

"Nobody likes to talk about their problems, Javier. But that's what friends are for, to help other friends with problems."

"I'm so glad you're here, Abuelita. I've missed talking to you. You're so wise. You really know a lot of important things about life."

"I'm not very wise, but I have lived for a long time. And I plan to keep living awhile longer," Abuelita said with a laugh.

"That's good," said Javier. "Now I'm going to call Lupe and tell her you're here. But I'm not going to tell her that I have a plan to buy Spider's car."

"You keep secrets from her, already?" asked Abuelita with a smile.

Javier smiled back at his grandmother.

11. A Surprise

Time passed. Javier got a job at a local supermarket. He was working as a box boy. He liked his job because he was earning good money. Sometimes he helped people carry groceries to their cars. Sometimes they gave him tips. The job wasn't difficult and it gave Javier many chances to practice his English. As he helped the customers to their cars, he often practiced English with the English speaking customers.

Javier worked after school four days a week. Once in awhile, Lupe came to visit him at the supermarket. She was happy he was working. She sometimes waited for him to get off work and then they walked home together. As they walked, they planned their future.

"You know, Lupe," said Javier, "pretty soon I'm going to be able to drive you home. I'll have a beautiful Chevy and we'll go everywhere."

"Javier, I don't mind walking," said Lupe. "I like to walk. When we walk, everything is slower and I like that. This city moves too fast for me. Besides, you won't have enough money to buy a car for a long time."

"You're wrong, Lupita. You know I'm saving my salary and my tips, but I'm also working on a special surprise."

"What is it, Javier? Are you keeping a secret from me?"

"Well, yes. I have a little surprise in the works. Come over to my house for a few minutes and I'll show you."

"Okay, Javier," answered Guadalupe. "But I'd better call my mother and tell her where I am."

"She knows you're with me, your *novio*," he smiled. "But you can call her from my house. I want you to see what I'm doing, okay?"

"Okay, Javier. Besides, I want to see your grandmother, your Abuelita again. It's always fun talking with her."

They walked more quickly to Javier's house. When they arrived, Abuelita greeted Javier and Guadalupe. She was glad to see Guadalupe again. Abuelita thought that Javier had a lovely girlfriend.

"Good afternoon, Abuelita," said Javier and Guadalupe.

"Abuela, don't tell her about the surprise! I want to show her myself." Javier went out of the room. When he returned, he was carrying a small wooden box. It had a rose carved into the top.

"That's a very pretty box, Javier," said Guadalupe.

"I think so, too," said Abuelita. "Javier made it. His father is teaching him how to make boxes and how to carve flowers into them."

Guadalupe was surprised. "You made this box, Javier? And you carved the rose?"

Javier felt shy. "It wasn't difficult, Lupe. I've made three boxes already. It doesn't take me very long and I enjoy doing it. It's really fun. When I started, my father helped me. He showed me how to do it and we worked together. Now I can do it by myself. I listen to music and work with my knife." He brought the other two boxes to show her.

"They're so pretty, Javier," said Guadalupe.

"One of them is for you, Guadalupe," said Javier.

"Really? Which one?" asked Guadalupe.

"Whichever one you want. You choose the one you want," said Javier.

Now Guadalupe felt shy. She didn't know which box to choose. They were all different and all pretty. She liked each one. She was happy Javier had made one for her. She was also happy that he was learning to carve. Carving was a fine craft, she thought. "Thank you, Javier. I think I'd like the box with the rose carved on top."

"I'm glad you chose that one. I thought you would like it the best," said Javier.

"But I like them all, Javier," said Guadalupe.

"I'm going to sell the other wooden boxes at the swap meet. Then I'll have more money to buy my car. I'm going to try to make enough boxes by Sunday to really earn some money."

"You know," Guadalupe said, "I need to think of a way to help you with those lovely boxes. Maybe I can paint designs on the outside of the ones you don't carve. I'll have to practice."

"That's a very good idea," said Abuelita, "then you two could work on the boxes together. You might even work while you're at the swap meet selling the boxes. When it isn't crowded with customers, you could paint boxes. By the way, I'd like to go to this swap meet, too. When is it?"

"Oh, there's a swap meet twice a month, on Sundays. People sell whatever they have: new things, old things, antiques, junk, whatever. They have it in the parking lot of the college, over there," explained Javier.

"I go with my mother every month," said Guadalupe. Then, all of a sudden, she remembered something important. "Oh no! I forgot to call my mother. I'd better hurry home. She'll be worried about me. I hope she won't be angry."

Guadalupe picked up her special wooden box and ran out the door. "Good-bye everybody," she called. "Good-bye, Abuelita, good-bye, Javier."

"Good-bye, Lupe," they called after her.

12. A Gang Problem

The swap meet was great! Javier sold all the boxes he had carved. Lupe also painted one of the boxes in the morning and sold it in the afternoon. They enjoyed taking turns walking around and looking at all the different things people were selling. Abuelita was with them. She enjoyed walking around and seeing what was for sale. They all liked bargaining for good prices at the swap meet. Abuelita spent a little money and Javier earned some money, so everyone had a good time.

Javier and Lupe had to pack up their display tables and go home in the late afternoon. On the way home, Javier and his grandmother dropped Lupe off at her house. Then, they went home. Javier parked his father's car and began to unload the display tables. His mother came out of the house.

"Javier," she called. "Spider is on the phone. It's the third time he's called you in the last fifteen minutes. It sounds like he really needs to speak to you."

Javier got a strange feeling in his stomach. As he ran to talk to Spider, his mind was racing. He knew that if Spider had called three times in fifteen minutes, there was a problem. He knew Spider was having problems. He was worried. He quickly picked up the phone and tried to sound calm.

"Hey, Spider, what's up?" asked Javier.

For a short second, there was silence at the other end of the line. Then, Spider spoke. "Javier, my friend, listen to me. You've got to listen to me."

"Hey, Spider, what's wrong? You sound bad. You sound terrible. What's going on?" asked Javier, still trying to sound calm.

"It's bad. It's my brother. One of the other gangs drove by our house. My brother was outside waxing his car. They shot him. I don't know why, but they shot him. I know they're going to come back. I need your help."

"You've got it. What do you need, my friend?" asked Javier.

"I need you to drive me over to their place. In my car. I just want to talk to them," said Spider.

Javier had a strange feeling in his stomach again. He knew that there was going to be trouble. "I'll be over there right away, Spider," Javier said in a quiet, low voice.

"No, I'll come pick you up," said Spider. "Right now, okay?"

"Right," agreed Javier.

When he hung up the telephone, he tried to appear calm. He did not want to worry his family. But everyone knew that if Spider was calling, there was a problem. A gang problem. When Javier turned around, his father, his mother, his sister, and his grandmother were all standing, waiting to hear what had happened.

"I need to help Spider," explained Javier. "I'm going to drive him to his friend's house."

"What for? Why does he need you to drive him, Javier? Why can't he drive himself? What's going on?" asked Mr. Flores.

"Well, I don't exactly know, but I'm going to drive his car. He asked me to drive it for him," said Javier.

"Is he going with you?" asked Mr. Flores.

"Yes," said Javier.

"Why can't he drive himself?" asked Mr. Flores in a worried voice. "You don't need to drive him anywhere. I don't want you to get into any trouble. Spider is probably having trouble with a gang and that is none of our business."

"Your father is right, Javier. We don't want any trouble," added Mrs. Flores.

"Just a minute, here," interrupted Abuelita. "Javier is trying to be a good friend. Maybe his friend Spider *is* in a gang and having a gang problem. If this is true, then we have to help him. That's what friends are for. Come on, Javier, let's go."

Javier and his grandmother started to leave.

"You can't go with him, Abuelita. This could be very dangerous," said Mr. Flores.

"That's exactly why I must go. When there is danger, we must all be brave and stick together. That's what makes a strong family. Now let's hurry, Javier."

Javier and his grandmother quickly ran outside. They saw the red Chevy coming up the street. Spider was driving fast. He screeched to a stop. Javier and his grandmother started to get in the car.

"Wait a minute, man," said Spider. "What's your Abuelita doing?" Spider looked pale and frightened.

"She's coming with us. She knows a lot about gangs and gang problems. It's okay, Spider. Believe me."

Spider didn't say anything. He wasn't feeling too good. Abuelita got in the back seat. Spider moved over to the passenger seat. "You're driving, right?" he asked Javier. Javier got in behind the wheel.

"Right. I'm driving." Javier looked up and saw his family looking out of the house. They looked very worried as they watched Spider's Chevy drive away.

13. A Gang Confrontation

"Where's your brother now?" Abuelita asked Spider as they sped to their destination.

"One of his friends took him to the hospital. My mother is there, too. She's been crying a lot. And she's worried."

"Of course, she's worried," said Abuelita. "And you need to help her stop worrying. You can help her and your brother."

"I don't know if I can help," Spider said, "but I'm going to let these guys know what's up. They shot my brother."

"Do you know why they shot your brother?" asked Abuelita.

"Oh, you know. It's one gang against another. That's why. That's it. That's the whole reason!"

"But killing doesn't help anything. Killing makes everything worse. We are fighting against each other and not going anywhere. We are killing our own brothers and sisters, for what? For what?"

"Listen, Abuelita, I know you're a good lady, and all of that, but my brother was shot and I've got to do something. You understand?" asked Spider.

"Yes, I understand. And I agree. You have got to do something. That's why I came along."

"Abuelita, you don't understand," interrupted Javier. "This is dangerous. Somebody might get shot. You shouldn't have come with us."

"Believe me, even if somebody gets shot, even if I get shot, we have to stop killing each other for no reason. And to do this, we have to work together, not one gang against another, but together."

But Spider had stopped listening. They were getting close to their destination.

"Turn left up there, Javier, and go straight for about a half a block. Drive slowly. It's the place on the right, the one with the black pickup truck in front of it." Spider continued, "Pull over and park, Javier." Spider was beginning to sound nervous. Javier was nervous, too. But Abuelita remained calm in the back seat.

There was nobody outside. Spider started to get out of the car. Javier watched him and saw him check a pistol that was hidden under his belt. Javier took a deep breath, trying to stay calm.

"Where are you going?" asked Abuelita.

"I'm just going to check things out," answered Spider.

"Just wait here. They'll come out, whoever they are. They know you want revenge for your brother. But they also know they didn't kill him. So they aren't too worried. They'll be out soon," said Abuelita.

"How do you know about this stuff, Abuelita?" asked Javier.

"I've been around for a long time. I've been watching people fight for years. There are people fighting in countries all over the world. Some people keep fighting; others look for peaceful solutions. I'm always looking for peaceful solutions," she answered.

"Shh . . . quiet," whispered Spider, "here they come."

Two young men were walking out of the building. As they walked toward the car, Abuelita opened her door. One of the men, looking surprised, reached for his gun.

"You two stay in the car unless I call you," said Abuelita, to Spider and Javier.

Abuelita walked up to the two young men. One of them had his gun pointed at her. She continued to walk toward them. Spider, in the car, had taken his gun out and was covering her from the car. Abuelita said in a loud voice,

"You can all put your pistols away. I'm here to talk with you, only to talk."

The young man slowly relaxed his gun. From the car Spider and Javier could not hear what Abuelita was saying, but they saw that the men were carefully listening to her. Spider wanted to know what Abuelita was saying. He wanted to know what was going on. He jumped out of the car and began running toward the young men talking to Abuelita.

"I know you shot my brother," he shouted angrily. "You tried to kill him. Who do you think you are? I'm going to kill you. Do you hear me? And now I am going to kill you!"

"No, you're not, Spider. Not unless you kill me first," said Abuelita moving and standing in front of the two young men. I don't want to die, but I'm old enough, and I've lived long enough. None of you has lived at all. Don't you want to live to be fathers, to be grandfathers, to be old with your grandchildren? Now stop this. You must stop this gang madness. I know one of these young men shot your brother. But if you shoot him, then everything will only get worse. And what do you get? Nothing but more pain, more problems. Right here, right now, we're going to talk," continued Abuelita. "Put down the guns."

The young men all looked at each other.

"She's right," said one of the gang members. "We should listen to her."

And they did. They talked, and yelled, and screamed, and cried. For a long time. And when it was over, they finally shook hands. But it wasn't over; it was only a beginning.

Spider drove Javier and Abuelita home. On the way home, Abuelita didn't speak much. She was very tired. She only said, "We must continue, this is only a beginning."

14. New Beginnings

Javier entered his senior year at high school. He didn't have to take English as a Second Language (ESL) classes in his senior year. English was still difficult but he had finished ESL. Now, he had to read long books in English and write compositions in many classes. There were still many words he didn't know, and writing sentences to express himself in English was a big problem. But with hard work, he could do it. He had learned a lot of English in school and at the swap meet. Luckily, Lupe often helped him with his English class.

Javier spent a lot of time with Lupe. They were always making plans for everything. They shared a booth at the swap meet twice a month. They worked hard preparing what they sold and many people came to their booth to buy the painted and carved boxes. While they sat in the booth, Javier and Lupe talked over all their plans. Javier planned to carve all kinds of different things out of wood—animals, birds, even lamps. Lupe could paint them and they would sell them at the swap meet.

They were saving money. Soon, Javier would have his own car. They wanted to get married, but they were waiting for the right time. Lupe wanted to go to the university. She was planning to be an accountant. Javier still didn't know what he wanted to be. He was planning to attend community college after high school graduation.

Spider wasn't planning but he was staying in school; he wasn't dropping out. Sometimes Spider studied with Radislav. And Spider was going to graduate. He was very proud of that.

At school, students could see that life had changed for Javier and Spider. Javier's sister, Ana, had told them about the gang shooting and Abuelita's courage. People knew that

Javier and Spider were more serious now, more grown-up. Abuelita held meetings with Spider's brother and other gang members. They were beginning to talk over their problems. They invited others to visit and discuss problems.

Abuelita also visited Javier's school to meet with the teachers and counselors. The teachers and counselors explained that many different cultural groups had problems and that everybody needed to work together toward a common peace. Abuelita saw that these were community problems. Everyone needed to come together to solve these problems. It was a big, but exciting task.

Javier had found his place in Los Angeles. His place was with his wonderful family, his girlfriend, his school friends, and his school. He knew that there was a life for him here. He could speak English and work hard. He could work with others to solve problems and plan. Plan for the future.

The End

Glossary of Terms

1. Javier /ha-vee-yer/; a man's name. In English, Xavier
2. Guadalajara /gwad-uh-la-ha-ra/; a city in the state of Jalisco
3. Jalisco /ha-lee-sko/; a state in Mexico
4. adobe /uh-do-bee/; earthen clay used for making houses and pottery
5. abuelita /a-bway-lee-ta/; Spanish for grandmother
6. señor /sen-yor/; Spanish for Mr. or sir
7. maestra /ma-ace-tra/; Spanish for teacher
8. Luz /looz/; a woman's name; Spanish for light
9. Guadalupe /gwad-uh-loo-pay/; a woman's name
10. Tagui /tag-wee/; a woman's name; in Armenian, queen
11. Chuy /choo-ee/; a nickname in Spanish
12. Radislav /rad-iss-lav/; a man's name
13. Byung /bee-yung/; a man's name
14. Lupe /loo-pay/; a nickname for Guadalupe
15. amigo /uh-mee-go/; Spanish for friend
16. novia /no-vee-uh/; Spanish for girlfriend
17. pandilla /pan-dee-ya/; Spanish for gang
18. novio /no-vee-o/; Spanish for boyfriend

CERTIFICATE OF COMPLETION
READING AWARD

This is to certify that _____ has completed *Javier Arrives in the U.S.: A Text for Developing Readers.*

CONGRATULATIONS!

You're on the road to successful reading. Keep up the good work!

_____ _____
Teacher's Signature   School   Date